T0329745

Short Selling

Short Selling

FINDING UNCOMMON SHORT IDEAS

Amit Kumar

Columbia Business School
Publishing

Columbia University Press
Publishers Since 1893
New York   Chichester, West Sussex
Copyright © 2015 Columbia University Press
All rights reserved

Library of Congress Cataloging-in-Publication Data
Kumar, Amit (Certified Financial Analyst)
[Short stories from the stock market]
Short selling: Finding uncommon short ideas / Amit Kumar.
pages cm
Originally published in 2012 as: Short stories from the stock market : uncovering
common themes behind falling stocks to find uncommon short ideas.
Includes bibliographical references and index.
ISBN 978-0-231-17224-0 (cloth : alk. paper) — ISBN 978-0-231-53884-8 (ebook)
1. Short selling. 2. Stocks—Prices. 3. Investments. I. Title.
HG6041.K86 2015
332.63'228—dc23

2015005506

Columbia University Press books are printed on permanent
and durable acid-free paper.
This book is printed on paper with recycled content.
Printed in the United States of America

COVER IMAGE:
© Getty Images / Mike Kemp

COVER DESIGN:
Milenda Nan Ok Lee

References to Internet Web sites (URLs) were accurate at the time of writing.
Neither the author nor Columbia University Press is responsible for URLs
that may have expired or changed since the manuscript was prepared.

To my Guru, family, friends, and clients
—my sources of strength.

Contents

Contents

Preface

Word of Caution!

Short selling is not for the faint of heart. While fortunes have been made shorting, many have also been lost. Shorting stocks is for the financially experienced and sophisticated investors with a strong stomach for losses. It can be potentially very dangerous to your wealth. Although this book may be a helpful guide to finding successful short ideas, when it comes to actually shorting them, you are on your own. Please consult with your financial advisor before taking any action.

Who Should Read This Book?

The book provides a research framework for individual and professional investors, finance students and professors, stock market reporters, and other stock enthusiasts to find uncommon short ideas and avoid common traps and hot stocks. Investors and professional analysts will find this book useful to uncover and pitch new short ideas.

Finance students seeking careers as professional analysts can benefit from this book. Finance professors can draw upon various examples and the shorting framework in the book to complement traditional textbooks on equity analysis. Market reporters, stock bloggers, and other stock market enthusiasts will find the book useful to watch for common themes behind short ideas that may have been overlooked by the stock market.

Why Should You Read This Book?

There is a natural psychological bias toward buying stocks. The Dow Jones Industrial Average (DJIA) has continued rising from the 100 range in the 1920s to the 14,000 range in 2007, generating a compounded annual return of around 6 percent. Shorting stocks against this backdrop may seem like sailing against the tide. Rising tides often lift even the least sail-worthy boats.

Short sellers have profited from less worthy stocks since the 1600s, when exchange-based trading began in Amsterdam; however, books on short selling are few and far between. Good investment books expound on downside risks in long ideas; however, risk analysis can always find one risk or another with any long idea.

Shorting stocks is not exactly the opposite of buying stocks, and risk analysis of long ideas may not always detect clear signals to short. It takes more to uncover short ideas. I present a short selling framework in this book that uncovers the common themes behind falling stocks to find uncommon short ideas.

While shorting is inherently risky, investors can profit from well-researched short ideas. When a short thesis points out problems endemic to a specific industry, investors can short both stocks and sector funds in that industry to beat market returns.

While investors may not always choose to act on short ideas, they can still avoid losses by using this framework to analyze weaknesses in their existing portfolio.

Structure of the Book and Content

I have divided the book into three parts: Part I lays out the framework to identify short opportunities. Chapter 1 explains the risks of shorting based only on high valuations and lays out a more comprehensive framework to identify shorts. Chapter 2 explains the inherent risks with leveraged businesses and the operating metrics that lead to a short idea. Chapter 3 describes issues with business models and turns in growth stories that can drive down stocks. Chapter 4 points out issues with key financial assumptions that can raise red flags about the business. Chapter 5 explains that history can be a good compass to navigate an ongoing crisis and that recession and crises can result in tightening credit cycles that expose vulnerabilities in certain business models.

Part II examines investment frameworks and public recommendations by reputed investors as sources of short ideas. Chapter 6 delves into the value investing principles originally formulated by Ben Graham and the perspective of value investors on short selling. It also contains an exclusive interview with noted value investor, Jean-Marie Eveillard. Chapter 7 walks through the history of activist investing and contains an exclusive interview with Bill Ackman, a reputed activist investor and short seller. Chapter 8 illustrates examples of when it may be useful to bet with or against reputed investors and when to stay away. Chapter 9 contains an exclusive interview with Mark Roberts and samples of Off Wall Street research on short ideas.

Part III describes the risks and mechanics of shorting. Chapter 10 considers when to hold or fold your position and provides examples of mistakes, traps, and hot stocks to avoid. Chapter 11 describes the mechanics of short selling and how short selling is not the opposite of buying stocks.

I have used case studies throughout the book to illustrate the shorting framework in practice. I have drawn examples from my past research as well as research contributed by Off Wall Street, a short-focused research firm with a successful track record that spans two decades.

Acknowledgments

I would like to thank a number of friends who read early versions of my book and provided their valuable feedback. I am grateful to Jereme Axelrod, Pankaj Nevatia, Ajay Singh, Pallav Gupta, Vinodh Nalluri, and Amit Gupta for giving useful and detailed suggestions.

Special thanks to Mark Roberts from Off Wall Street for his exclusive interview for this book. I am also grateful to Mark for sharing some of his exceptional past work in researching short ideas. Many thanks to Jean-Marie Eveillard for sharing his insights on value investing.

I would like to thank Bill Ackman for taking the time to read the first edition of the book and sharing his valuable feedback, as well as agreeing to interview for the current edition.

I owe thanks to my professors at Columbia Business School: Bruce Greenwald, whose framework on barriers to entry in an industry is immensely useful; and Suresh Sundaresan, whose lectures on advance derivatives went over my head in the classroom, but shortly after helped me make sense of the ensuing financial crisis.

Acknowledgments

I also want to thank the great investors who visited Columbia Business School and lent their insights, shared their mistakes, and took questions. Their lectures shaped my research process and helped me to understand the psychology of investing. Special thanks to Jim Chanos, whose lecture helped me see the distinction between going long and selling short.

Last but not least, I am thankful to my wife for her loving support.

Deep appreciation to my daughter, who eagerly asked every day, "Is your book ready, Dad?" and kept me inspired to complete the book. To my parents, brothers, and family—thank you for your confidence and support.

PART I

Framework to Finding Short Ideas

Due Diligence in Short Selling

It's common for promoters to cause a stock to become valued at
5 to 10 times its true value, but rare to find a stock trading at 10
to 20percent of its true value. So you might think short selling
is easy, but it's not.
— WARREN BUFFETT

ENRON IS A POSTER CHILD for accounting fraud and financial
shenanigans. Jim Chanos, an early short seller of Enron in 2001,
first noticed the stock in a *Wall Street Journal* article on gain-on-sale
accounting practices at large energy trading firms. In congressional testimony, he said that he became interested in Enron because
the gain-on-sale approach allowed management to estimate future
profitability and tempted them to create earnings out of thin air.[1]

In his meeting with Wall Street analysts, Chanos had found that
their buy ratings were not backed by analysis and were marred by
conflicts of interest. These ominous signs, coupled with Enron's
rich valuation, made Enron a perfect short for Chanos. Short sellers like Chanos have played the role of the canary in the coal mine
for the stock market.

A few years later in 2007, John Paulson, who ran an epony-
mous hedge fund, made billions of dollars betting against subprime mortgages. Paulson told a congressional committee that he
had conducted detailed independent research in 2005 and 2006
to conclude that mortgage securities were completely mispriced.[2]

He believed that many AAA-rated investment-grade securities would become worthless because their underlying collaterals comprised subprime mortgages that were made with 100 percent financing and no down payment. Paulson, like other successful short sellers who bet against subprime, believed that financial firms such as Lehman Brothers, Bear Stearns, and AIG ran into trouble because they had excessive leverage.

Paulson noted that Lehman Brothers had more than 40 times the assets compared to their tangible common equity (Lehman was basically trying to carry many times its own body weight). Equity at many financial firms was too thin to absorb losses from their exposure to subprime mortgages and related complex derivatives. The subprime crisis began to unfold in March 2007, when New Century Financial Corporation, the second-largest U.S. subprime lender, reached the brink of collapse.

Our delegation from Columbia Business School was visiting Warren Buffett in Omaha that month, and I had the opportunity to seek his opinion on the ongoing fears of a housing crisis. Buffett told me that the market was panicking for good reason, and the fear of an impending subprime crisis was very real because homeowners were not making their mortgage payments. Buffett benefited from his own clairvoyance by buying companies in distress during the ensuing financial crisis; however, he did not short stocks.

On the contrary, Buffett sold long-term equity puts on S&P 500 companies; that is, he promised to buy the market index if it fell substantially over the next ten to fifteen years. Buffett was no stranger to short selling when he ran his partnership from 1957 to 1968. His partnership generated 26 times return (precisely 2610.6 percent), mainly from buying stocks; however, he also shorted companies in early Berkshire years.[3]

So, why doesn't Buffett short now?

Buffett manages approximately $100 billion of stock investments for Berkshire Hathaway. He can find very few long (forget short) ideas that fit the size of his bets because he likes to make

4

concentrated bets. He can raise his bets on longs when the stock moves against him, but he cannot raise his bets on shorts. Concentrated shorts can be disastrous and do not meet his risk parameters.

Like Buffett, hedge funds also tend to make outsized bets on long ideas because longs are usually more rewarding than shorts. They like to rely on their own proprietary research, but they also have access to a plethora of long ideas from Wall Street analysts, company management teams, and other sources.

A hedge fund incentive structure typically consists of 2 percent management fees and 20 percent of the profit-sharing arrangement with the client. Unlike long-only managers who strive to beat index benchmark returns, hedge funds strive to deliver absolute returns regardless of the market conditions. Delivering absolute returns in a bear market is impossible without a short-selling product for hedge funds. How else can they "hedge" the downside risk in a bear market after all? Their clients are willing to share part of their profit in return for the hope of an absolute return.

The hedge fund investment mandate requires them to short stocks and hedge their long bets. It takes longer to research short ideas because hedge funds look for early negative information that may not be readily available. There is also a dearth of short-focused stock research firms. Therefore, hedge funds and other money managers typically entertain short ideas more than long ideas, especially if they are on the long, or possibly wrong, side of the trade. It is always possible for hedge funds to find overvalued stocks, and you might wonder why it is not easy for them to simply short stocks with high valuation.

Sell High, Buy Low: Are Companies with High Valuation Good Shorts?

Although buying low and selling high usually works for long ideas, selling short based only on high valuation usually does not work as well. Investment theses for short ideas work well when a company faces clear issues with its business model, whereas high valuation only serves as icing on the cake. Let us take a look at how companies are valued in order to understand why a high valuation is not enough to make a good short play.

While there are many approaches and metrics to value a firm, the basic idea of valuation boils down to either earnings or cash flow potential of the firm or the value of assets owned by the firm. Market expectations for revenues, earnings, cash flow, and asset values drive the stock price of the firm. Higher expectations drive up valuation multiples (see text box, "P/E/ Valuation 101").

The market can be maniacally ebullient, causing wide-ranging and long-lasting anomalies in stock prices compared to their fair valuations. Although you can hold on to your long ideas during this turbulence, you will most likely be forced to cover your short position by the lender when the pricey short keeps rising. Therefore, it may not be a good idea to short based only on high valuations.

As an example, two firms that earned $1 per share last year may be priced at $10 per share and $30 per share, respectively, depending on market expectations for their future earnings. Firm A, which is priced at $30 (or a P/E of 30), is expected to earn much more than firm B, which is priced at $10 (or a P/E of 10). Let us assume that firm A grows its earnings from $1 to $3 over the next two years, whereas firm B continues to earn $1 per share. At this point, if the market believes that firm A has reached its full earnings potential and decides to pay a P/E of 10 (the same as firm B) for firm A, the stock price for firm A will stay put at $30.

In this case, if we shorted firm A simply because it was trading at a high multiple, we would have underestimated the firm's growth potential and the short trade would lose money or break even, at best. In a more bullish case, firm A will continue to command a premium multiple if markets believed that firm A could keep growing its earnings at the same rate for another couple of years. The short trade would lose money in this case.

The price-to-earnings ratio (P/E) or the ratio of stock price to earnings per share (EPS) is the most commonly used valuation metric. A P/E multiple of 10 means that the investor is willing to pay $10 per share per $1 of last year's EPS.

Let us consider a simple question. If your bank promises a 5 percent per year deposit rate for the rest of your life, how much would you need to deposit to earn $10,000 per month (or $120,000 per year)? The answer is $2.4 million. In this case, the value of your investment ($2.4 million) is 20 times the annual earnings ($120,000 per year). Simply put, the P/E on your investment is 20; that is, you are willing to pay 20 times every dollar in interest income at the bank because the expected rate of return (or yield) is 5 percent per year.

There is an extremely low likelihood that you will lose your deposits at the bank. Investments in treasuries (government bonds), investment-grade corporate bonds, and money market funds bear a low risk of loss as well; however, such investments are riskier than simple bank deposits.

Investors expect higher rates of return (or yields) on higher risk investments than deposits and will pay lower multiples. Stocks are riskier than bonds, so their expected rates of return will be even higher. If a stock trades at $20 per share and the market expects the earnings to remain constant at last year's EPS of $2, the earnings yield is 2/20 (10 percent) and the P/E multiple is 20/2 (10 times).

Now, if the market expects the EPS to double every year for the next three years, would the market still pay a P/E multiple of 10? In this case, the company will earn $4, $8, and $16 or a total of $28 over the next three years (higher than the current stock price). If most earnings flow to their cash balance (remember that companies report earnings on an accrual basis, not on a cash basis), they can theoretically go private by buying back all their shares in 2.5 years.

In general, low P/E indicates that the market expects a lower earnings level, and high P/E indicates that the market expects growth in earnings. The P/E for a company with growth expectations will be much higher than 10 and can reach ridiculous levels (100 to 500), depending on hype and the market sentiment.

It is important to understand the drivers of sustainable growth (total addressable market for the product, unique features of the product, competitive dynamics, product shelf life, time needed for a competitor to design and bring alternative or competitive products to the market) and clear reasons or catalysts that could derail the growth trajectory. It is not a good idea to short a company with open-ended growth that is hard to estimate. Such shorts are more often wrong than right.

During the dot-com bubble of the late 1990s, companies with no history of sales traded on multiples of hope, and it seemed that the valuation methods for traditional industries did not apply to the new-world technology companies. Even technology companies with demonstrable sales, such as Cisco, traded at insane multiples. Enterprise value to sales or price to sales are the most commonly used valuation metrics for fast-growing technology companies.

In July 1998, Cisco reported annual revenues of $8.5 billion—30 percent higher than the prior year due to increasing unit sales of high-end switches—and the stock traded close to 10x sales for a market cap of approximately $85 billion. A year later in July 1999, Cisco reported a 40 percent increase in sales to $12.1 billion, and it traded at approximately 20x sales for a market cap of approximately $210 billion.[4] In July 1999, did Cisco's valuation seem extended, projecting sales to continue growing at 40 percent for many years? Maybe, but Cisco's performance over the next year demonstrated the dangers of shorting based on valuation alone (figure 1.1).

In July 2000, Cisco reported a 60 percent increase in sales to $19 billion from continued growth in switches and routers sales. Cisco was now trading close to 25x sales for a market cap of more than $450 billion. In terms of P/E, Cisco was trading at a P/E of approximately 200, up from a P/E of 90 in 1999. A short trade at a P/S of 20 or a P/E of 90 would have resulted in a negative 110 percent return, and a concentrated short bet on Cisco could have destroyed the investor's portfolio. As John Maynard Keynes

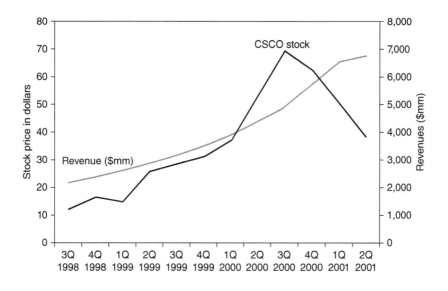

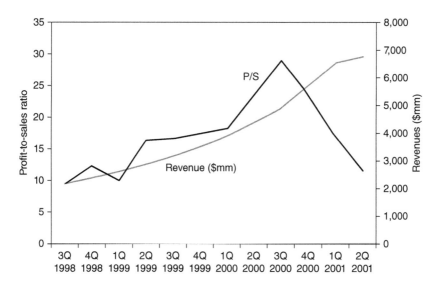

FIGURE 1.1 Cisco revenues, stock price, P/S 1998–2001. *Source:* Cisco SEC filings.

is often quoted as having said, "Markets can remain irrational longer than you can remain solvent." Keynes, like Ben Graham, suffered a huge blow to his investments during the 1929 crash; his quote is a stark reminder that capital misallocation can lead to disastrous portfolio returns.

Hindsight is 20/20. It is easy to see why it would have been wise to sell Cisco at a P/S of 25 in 2000 and not at 20 in 1999. When Cisco's revenues were growing 40 to 50 percent annually, it was hard to estimate addressable market for switches and routers; it was also hard to predict whether Cisco would remain the technology leader in the market. Cisco's gross margins could also have kept growing with operating scale. Frequent merger and acquisition (M&A) transactions could further confound Cisco's growth estimates. If we had a crystal ball to predict market size, it would still be impossible to guess the *most insane multiple* that the market would be willing to pay for Cisco stock.

The Cisco story illustrates the typical timing difficulty in shorting growth or high valuation stocks. Nonetheless, if we can spot flaws in the business model of such companies or identify catalysts that can permanently hurt their growth prospects, high valuation can be a good starting point to look for short ideas.

Takeaway
Shorting expensive stocks based only on valuation is dangerous.

Researching the Short Idea Requires the Same Fundamental Skills as Those for Longs

Fundamental research can uncover flaws with business models. Fundamental analysis for possible short positions is not different from that for long positions, which involves understanding business models, analyzing financial statements, identifying growth drivers of business and industry, valuing businesses, evaluating downside risks, and finding an edge on the investment thesis.

Such investment classics as *Security Analysis* by Ben Graham, *Essays of Warren Buffett*, and *Common Stocks and Uncommon Profits* by Phil Fisher provide excellent frameworks for fundamental analysis of businesses and lend insight into the minds of successful value investors. Similarly, *One Up on Wall Street* by Peter Lynch and investment letters from growth investors provide frameworks (e.g., sizing the market, analyzing ongoing trends, and growth potential for new products) to analyze compounders or growth companies and find conviction in their growth prospects.

It is important to understand the reinvestment economics of a company to identify the levers of growth. Companies in growth markets tend to invest in product research and development, distribution capacity (e.g., stores, warehouses), manufacturing capacity, brand marketing, or sales force expansion. Each of these investments allows a company to increase or capture market share; however, such reinvestments in the business may not necessarily result in profitable growth.

It is critical to look at the following seven aspects of any business, which is by no means an exhaustive list but is a good checklist for fundamental analysis.

Checklist for Fundamental Analysis

1. Industry: Market size, market concentration (top-five market share), competition, nature of the industry (capital intensity, seasonality, etc.), stage of the industry (nascent, mature, etc.), signs of cyclical or structural changes in the industry

2. Product: Unique features and competitiveness, research and development investments, marketing investments, scalability, customer captivity, switching cost, substitutes, product moats (patent protection, regulatory barriers, etc.)

3. Financial statements analysis and valuation:

   (a) Mature businesses

      Income statement: Revenue drivers, fixed and variable costs, last ten-year earnings before interest and taxes (EBIT)/operating margins, net income, and returns on equity/capital, quality of earnings, and cyclicality/seasonality in the business

      Balance sheet: Investment asset quality and liquidity, leverage and covenants, balance sheet line items (inventory/working capital, etc.)

      Cash flows: Reasons behind convergence/divergence from earnings, capital expenditures (Capex), and financing

   (b) New businesses: Drivers of revenue and earnings growth, sources and usage of cash, and cash burn rate, plus any additional relevant metrics mentioned for mature businesses above, where available

   (c) Valuation: Relevant valuation multiple for the industry, such as price to book, P/E, price to sales (P/S), enterprise value to sales (EV/sales), enterprise value to EBIT (EV/EBIT), EV/(EBITDA − Capex), net asset value, discounted cash flow, free float, free funds flow, and free cash flow multiples, etc.

4. Customers: Export versus domestic sales percent of revenue, customer concentration (customers with >5–10

percent of revenue), company's position and competitive strength in the industry value chain

5. Management team: History of execution, shareholder value creation, capital allocation, reputation, ethics, insider ownership and executive compensation, recent insider transactions

6. Economic cycle of the business: Current economic state, cyclicality, seasonality, growth cycle, current growth stage, monetary cycles, and currency movements

7. Near-term and long-term threats: Legal, product cycle/ substitutes, competition, regulatory/sovereign risk, structural changes in business model, patent expirations, waning product demand

Structural Shorts, Tactical Shorts, and Paired Shorts

Before digging into the due diligence process behind short ideas, let me classify shorts into three categories with different investment horizons: (1) structural shorts, with a one- to two-year outlook; (2) tactical shorts, with a one-week to one-quarter outlook; and (3) paired shorts, where investors hedge longs with temporary shorts on the stock's competitors, vendors, clients, etc. The due diligence process for each of these categories is not equally rigorous.

In general, a successful structural short thesis can point at cracks in the business model, structural changes in the industry, financial shenanigans, changing competitive landscape, abnormally high valuations, peak operating margins, and most importantly, multiple impending short-term negative catalysts. I would also include cyclical shorts in this category because most long-term issues appear to be cyclical issues first and eventually become chronic.

Tactical shorts are typically short-term trades based purely on speculation, momentum (short a falling stock ex-post negative news), and sympathy trades (e.g., speculation on a slowdown in the luxury segment after negative news from a luxury brand and short other stocks in the luxury-brand sector). Some high-frequency trading firms also use proprietary quantitative strategies to short stocks and hold short positions anywhere between a few milliseconds to a full day. I will not cover tactical shorting based on technical or quantitative analysis or chart reading beyond the concept of *peak-to-trough corrections*.

Paired shorts, as the name suggests, are combinations of long and short trades, such as short Boeing and long EADS (two companies in the same industry) or short Corning and long Best Buy (short supplier and long customer). Generally, the motivation behind pair trades is to hedge systemic risks of long trades; such short trades tend to be sloppy and not as well researched as their long counterparts. Analysts can source such short ideas from a headline on a short thesis from a newspaper, a friend, Wall Street, and even their shoe shiner, among other sources.

In this chapter, I focus on the due diligence process to find structural shorts based on the analysis of public filings and earnings or presentation transcripts. The analysis is focused on issues with their business model, such as declining demand for products and services, emergence of new product substitutes, rising input costs, threats from alternative distribution channels, declining profitability, and competitive pressure. As these issues evolve, investors try to find an edge through primary research before the issues find wider coverage in newspapers and other media.

Analysts rely on scuttlebutt (Phil Fisher popularized this approach), channel checks, proprietary surveys, field trips, management interviews, idea dinners, and the like to improve their informational advantage on short ideas. However, some of these research tools can be resource intensive, expensive, and more suited for tactical shorting based on estimating the next quarterly sales, earnings, or cash flow.

Takeaway
Structural shorts are longer-term shorts on companies
with structural issues with their business or business
model. Tactical shorts focus on shorter-term issues and
rely on scuttlebutt, surveys, and channel checks.

Why Do Stocks Fall?

Let us take a look into some key reasons behind negative stock
price action and related stories. Some of these events and reasons
can prove to be prognostic indicators for a short thesis. None
of these may be reason alone to buy or short a stock, and there
is no shortcut to fundamental research for higher conviction in
short ideas. Sourcing short ideas is hard even for veteran short
sellers. The following catalysts covered within the short-selling
framework can help source and vet short ideas.

Investigations: Internal or Regulatory

Internal or regulatory investigation announcements are almost
always a negative surprise for the stock, especially if the investigations are announced on the heels of an already announced
negative news item or accusation against the company. Obvi-
ously, such investigations cannot be predicted; however, the odds
of an investigation increase dramatically if a reputed news source,
investor, or analyst presents compelling evidence of an accounting
misrepresentation or unethical business practice.

Typically, when such news breaks, the stock turns into a hot
stock, gyrating for a few days and igniting a tug of war between

SHORT-SELLING FRAMEWORK:
WHAT TO LOOK FOR

1. Structural shorts

    a. Unsustainable leveraged business model

        i.   Threat of covenant breach, credit rating downgrade
        ii. Decline in the value of assets financed by debt
        iii. Declining same-store sales, long-term operating leases
        iv. Heavy dependence on financing, tightening credit cycle

    b. Business model issues

        i.   Loss of key client, product, executive, or subsidies
        ii. Industry on a secular or cyclical declining trend
        iii. Signs of market share loss and threat to profit margins
        iv. Declining prices, rising raw material cost, or both
        v.   Government investigation of business practices, fraud
        vi. Mergers and acquisitions that kick issues down the road,
             expensive acquisitions
        vii. Exiting high-margin business or entering low-margin
             business resulting in a lower operating margin profile

    c. Value traps: Stocks that may seem cheap on certain metrics,
       but in reality may not have moats to protect their business
       and may face long-term chronic issues
    d. Broken growth stories: Strong competition, rival products
       from competitors or customers, products going out of fashion
    e. Financial statement issues and shenanigans

2. Tactical shorts

    a. Signs of macroeconomic issues and recession
    b. Successful investor announces a short position
    c. Initial public offering (IPO) lockup expiring, key investors
       exiting, insiders selling

3. Paired shorts: Short competitor or customer to hedge long position

bulls and bears. This may not be the best time to place a short trade, but it is a good time to research the stock to identify knock-on effects and other negative catalysts and related downside risk to the current valuation. In such a case, rich valuation may serve as icing on the cake.

In April 2011, Diamond Foods (DMND) announced a deal of approximately $2.4 billion to buy Pringles from P&G, including $1.5 billion in Diamond stock. Diamond had a market cap of approximately $1.3 billion, and this transformative deal would have doubled their 2011 sales. Six months later, *The Wall Street Journal* pointed out that Diamond had inflated their 2011 earnings by making a momentum payment to its walnut growers in September instead of July (the last month of their fiscal year). Diamond stock retreated from its all-time high as some noted short sellers began to point at serious flaws (see chapter 4) in Diamond's walnut business that could lower Diamond's gross margins and potentially threaten the Pringles deal.

After the news, Diamond was still trading at a rich valuation of a P/E of approximately 50 (standalone Diamond earnings) and a P/E of approximately 30, including the Pringles earnings. Diamond stock corrected approximately 17 percent from its high of $92 by mid-October after the *Wall Street Journal* article. On November 1, Diamond announced an internal investigation into the alleged accounting irregularity, resulting in a delay in closing the Pringles deal. The stock fell approximately 18 percent on the announcement.

On November 22, the death of a Diamond director who had recused himself from the internal investigation was reported as a suicide; Diamond stock plunged even further, by approximately 20 percent. The Securities and Exchange Commission (SEC) opened an investigation into the alleged irregularities. However, the Pringles deal was still on the table and the stock recovered approximately 35 percent to $37 by February 8, 2012.

On February 9, Diamond fired the chief executive officer (CEO) and chief financial officer after their initial internal investigation.

Diamond stock dove 37 percent on the news because the chances of a Pringle deal now appeared slim. On February 15, Kellogg announced a deal to buy Pringles, ending all speculation on the deal. Diamond stock subsequently fell another ~40 percent to $13 by November 19, 2012, as the company restated financials and struggled to repair its reputation.

In general, it is important to pay attention to investigations announced by the company or government regulatory agencies such as the Department of Justice, the Attorney General, the Federal Communications Commission, and the Federal Trade Commission. The announcements can sometimes lead to good short ideas, especially if the stock is trading at rich valuation multiples.

Investor Announcements and Insider Transactions

The market pays close attention to stock transactions by both outsiders (institutional investors and money managers) and insiders (company executives). Certain firms specialize in spotting unusual trends in such transactions, such as when key investors in a firm disclose significant increases or decreases in their stake, mostly by quietly filing a *Form 13* (F/D/H, etc.).

Executives or insiders can disclose their stakes through a *Form 4* filing, or planned stock sales through *Form 10b5* filings. Unusual or heavy insider selling can signal that insiders are aware of negative news that is unknown to the broader market. On December 10, 2012, *The Wall Street Journal* reported an insider-trading probe launched by Manhattan's Attorney General into cases where company executives sold their stocks (under *10b5* plan in many cases) prior to the announcement of material negative news.

In the case of IPOs and spin-offs, the initial owners and insiders are not allowed to sell their shares during an initial lockup period (typically 90 to 180 days preceding the public offering), and the lockup expiration calendar is publically available. The expiration dates are watched very closely because stock prices are expected to drop as a result of new supply entering the market.

Mostly, stocks react negatively to an exit of marquee or strategic investors and forewarnings from prominent short sellers. It is important to pay attention to float (shares available for trading) and short interest ratios (the number of shares sold short in the market as a percent of the float). Low float (concentrated ownership by a small number of investors) or a high short interest ratio (heavily shorted stocks) reduce the stock liquidity (ease in trading the stock) and cause wider swings in the stock price, or a short squeeze.

Short sellers are not required to disclose their stakes in the United States; however, they may choose to disclose their short position and make their pitch through public interviews and presentations. Most successful presentations point out clear flaws in a business model, accounting irregularities, or impending threats to the company's prospects to the extent that the short thesis seems to be a no-brainer. However, short sellers do not always expect such stocks to go to zero (even famous shorts on Enron and Lehman), and it is important to ensure that the current valuation allows a margin of safety for a short trade.

Short selling requires a contrarian mindset. Therefore, when a prominent investor takes a large long position in a cheap stock, it may be worthwhile to examine if the stock is a value trap. Finding a value trap is probably the hardest task. Not only do you need to deeply analyze the company's financial statements, but you also need to predict adverse demand trends for its product, broader industry, or macroeconomic indicators.

Last but not least, downgrades by sell-side analysts mostly result in a down day for stock. Short-term tactical calls are often based on channel checks or surveys conducted by the analysts. In some other cases, analysts might downgrade a stock on the heels of a poor earnings report or poor product launch, or after the stock is near their target price. It is usually difficult to source short ideas based on short-term tactical calls; however, longer-term calls that point to structural problems with a business can lead to good short ideas every once a while.

Loss of a Key Client, Product, Executive, or Subsidy

A company with revenues derived from the sale of one key product or sale to a key client naturally has a higher risk of mishaps and failure, akin to putting all of its eggs in one basket. The most common examples are biotechnology and pharmaceutical companies with a single drug. Among the many things that can go wrong for these companies, the drug may be coming off patent, insurance companies or Medicare reimbursement plans may drop coverage of the drug, the drug may cause unexpected side effects, clinical trials may not be successful, and alternative drugs may enter the market. In general, the risk in shorting companies with commercialized drugs is always much less than shorting companies with drugs in the pipeline.

CASE STUDY:
QUESTCOR PHARMACEUTICALS (QCOR)

In August 2007, Questcor Pharmaceuticals adopted a new pricing model for Acthar, its sole drug, used for the treatment of multiple sclerosis (MS) and infantile spasms. Questcor effectively raised the price of Acthar in 2007 from $1,650 per vial to $22,222 per vial. Questcor's revenues doubled over the next three years, from $49 million in 2007 to $115 million in 2010; the stock soared multifold, from $0.5 to approximately $15 by the end of 2010.[5]

Questcor was noticed by short sellers after the health care reform law required pharmaceutical companies to provide rebates to cover a portion of the Medicare Part D coverage gap, the so-called donut hole. Twenty-five percent of Questcor's sales came from Medicare-insured patients. Questcor responded by doubling its sales force to boost Acthar prescriptions for MS patients whose treatment was covered by commercial insurance companies. Consequently, prescriptions for MS increased to 3,090 from 1,212, boosting annual sales by 87 percent to $217 million in 2011 and doubling the stock price in 2011.

Short sellers were out of luck on this stock, and the tug of war between longs and shorts continued into 2012. In July 2012, a noted short seller argued that Acthar's active ingredient could be replicated in a generic version, sending the stock 23 percent lower. However, Questcor stock recouped its losses after it became eligible for lower Medicaid rebates in September 2012 (figure 1.2).

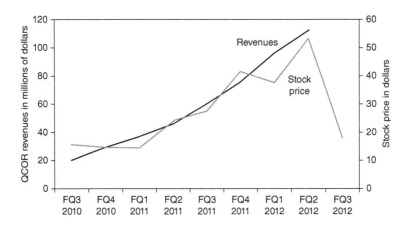

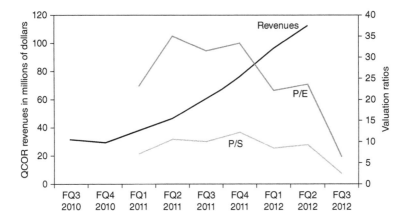

FIGURE 1.2 Questcor revenues, stock price, P/S, P/E 2010–2012.
Source: Questcor SEC filings.

The story was not over. Two weeks later, on September 18, 2012, Aetna published a clinical policy bulletin on Acthar to limit reimbursements to treatment of West syndrome (infantile spasms). QCOR fell nearly 50 percent on the news as the market worried that other insurers would follow suit. On the heels of this news, the SEC announced an investigation into Questcor's marketing practices. With a heavy short interest of 40 to 50 percent, QCOR was a hot stock. QCOR stock continued to remain depressed until it announced on June 12, 2013 that it would acquire the development and commercialization rights to Synacthen and Synacthen Depot from Novartis. On April 7, 2014, Mallinckrodt Pharmaceuticals announced that it would acquire Questcor for approximately $5.6 billion in cash and stock.

High-priced drugs often run into reimbursement issues from commercial insurers or Medicare, and their problems compound when a cheaper rival drug enters the market. In other cases, high-priced drugs may catch the attention of lawmakers. For example, Gilead Sciences faced scrutiny over its pricing strategy for Sovaldi, a hepatitis C drug that was approved only four months earlier on December 6, 2013. Although companies with diversified drug portfolios are less risky, single-drug companies are prone to getting out of businesses; the risk in their business model makes them more attractive candidates for short sellers.

Use of the single-product theme to identify short candidates applies to many other industries, such as smartphone makers. I want to quickly compare this industry with drug makers to point out additional issues with sustainable profitability for smartphone makers. Products such as smartphones are not as strongly protected by long-term patents as drug makers, and the design cycle for phones is much shorter than that of pharmaceuticals (drugs go through multiyear clinical trial processes).

A shorter product shelf life, design time, upgrade cycle, competition, and shifts in consumer trends make it hard for phone makers to profitably grow market share for more than two years. Once a phone maker loses luster for its hit product in the market, there seems no end to the decline in their revenues, such as in the cases of Motorola (unit sales fell 85 percent after their RAZR fallout in 2006), Nokia (unit sales fell more than 20 percent in 2010 as rival smartphones entered the market and Nokia entered a product recession), RIMM (unit sales fell more than 30 percent after product missteps in 2010), and HTC (unit sales fell more than 20 percent in 2011 on pricing missteps and competition).

Other Product Issues

Markets do not like uncertainties and they do not welcome negative headlines on profitability or growth prospects for a company, namely production and capacity expansion issues, supply chain disruptions, delays with product launch, excess inventory, input cost inflation, and so on. Sometimes, these headlines can point to broader and longer-term issues with the company.

CASE STUDY:
PILGRIM'S PRIDE CORPORATION (PPC)

Prices for corn and soybeans (key inputs for chicken farms) began rising in 2007 and hurt the margins of chicken producers. Their shares were down 20–30 percent from the peak in 2007. My fund manager had taken a long position in PPC and asked me to research the company.

Chicken producers had not hedged corn prices, and corn futures indicated more trouble coming for them. In particular, this was not good news for PPC, which had acquired Gold Kist for $1.3 billion, funded entirely by secured credit and bridge loans. Based on its 2007 earnings, PPC would have been required to pay a higher interest rate on its long-term debt because its debt/EBITDA ratio of 3.2 was above the restrictive covenant of 3.0.

Pilgrim's Pride spent approximately $2.4 billion on corn and soybean feedstock in 2007. If prices increased another 20–30 percent, as suggested by commodity futures, their cost of sales would have increased by an additional $400 million to $600 million. PPC could pass some of the cost to customers through price increases; however, historical data suggested that chicken prices rarely rose above 5 percent because consumers often shifted to beef. The chicken industry was already cutting production through 2007 after an oversupply in 2006. With plant utilization at 85 percent in 2007, drastic production increases seemed unlikely at PPC.

Pilgrim's Pride would have posted losses of at least $100 million in the best-case scenario of a 5 percent price increase, and they still could have risked breaching their debt covenants. They were also facing other cost issues related to fuel prices, labor shortages, and an increase in their interest rate on long-term debt. PPC seemed like a good short candidate; we sold our stake and went short. PPC posted significant losses in 2008 (figure 1.3) and filed for bankruptcy protection.

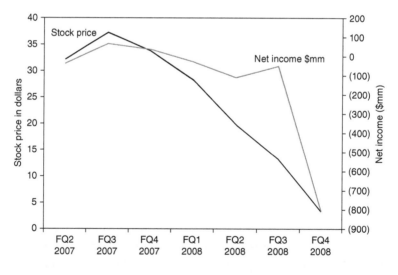

FIGURE 1.3 Pilgrim net income, stock price, corn price increase 2007–2008. *Source:* PPC SEC Filings, U.S. Department of Agriculture.

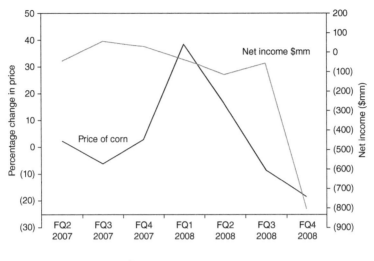

FIGURE 1.3 (*Continued*)

Industry Trends: Cyclical and Secular

When an industry begins to show signs of decline, it is important to understand whether the decline is secular, cyclical, or short term in nature. This aspect of investment research or analysis is an art, and there are no magic frameworks to understand and predict the nature of such trends. Industry experts, sell-side analysts, market research firms, and news media dedicate considerable resources to researching and publishing short-term and long-term themes and trends. Typically, short bets based on clear declining trends in an industry tend to be crowded trades that follow smart investors (or money).

When the advent of the Internet threatened traditional news dissemination, all newspaper stocks entered a multiyear decline period. Trends such as online delivery of content (video, audio, news, etc.) and outsourcing at the beginning of the twenty-first century have proved to be irreversible. Similar trends that promise cost benefits from comparative advantage can also last for many years. Other secular trends that emerge from shifts in consumer behavior, such as product obsolescence or substitution, disruptive technologies, and chronic overcapacity or oversupply (e.g., telecom bust), can also threaten long-term prospects of an industry or even lead to their demise.

Industries, just like companies, go through cycles of growth, maturity, or decline, and the profitability of companies within an industry is naturally correlated with the stage of the industry. During a growth phase, industries or companies can be financed by customers, capital markets, or government investments; these sources of funding eventually define their balance sheet characteristics. In general, hard-asset industries (e.g., airlines, banks, utilities) are heavily indebted, whereas soft-asset industries (e.g., services, software) tend to be financed by customers and remain free of debt.

The strength of a balance sheet or war chest can inject life into a company's ability to renovate and survive when its industry enters a cyclical or structural decline phase. However, when products offered by an industry become commoditized (e.g., personal computers [PCs]), it becomes hard even for companies with great balance sheets to reverse the decline in profitability; they become value traps for investors. Good managers can sometimes spot the declining trends early and decide to completely exit the business, such as when IBM decided to exit the PC business in 2004.

Exceptional managers can sometimes successfully retool the business. Steve Jobs steered Apple away from the PC business in 2004 to revolutionize digital music and the mobile phone industry. However, it is rare for even exceptional managers to be able to turn the tide of a secular decline. Dell was unable to reverse its decline despite its strong cash position and the return of its successful founder to the helm in 2007. Buffett probably saw many failed second acts from exceptional executives during his lengthy investing career. He captured this in one of his brilliant quotes: "When a management with a reputation of brilliance tackles a business with a reputation for bad economics, it is the reputation of the business that remains intact."

Financial Statement Issues

Uncovering accounting fraud is a dream job for short sellers, but it requires exceptional accounting forensic skills. Accounting forensics is no easy job; however, it is easy to pay attention to certain common issues, such as unusual divergence between sales and accounts receivable, high levels of inventory, asset valuations (changes in classification, mark-to-market assumptions, etc.), and major changes to accounting assumptions. Chapter 4 discusses some of the common accounting issues and related examples in more detail.

When a company discloses accounting problems, its stock is bound to fall as investors begin to question the integrity of its financial statements. Accounting problems can range from benign misclassifications to complex financial shenanigans. The most common scandals involve revenue recognition problems (to inflate sales), expense classifications (to understate costs), and masked liabilities (involving special-purpose entities and fake transactions).

Accounting is the language of business. Investing in a stock without reading its financial statements is akin to flying blind. Accounting issues are often symptoms of larger problems with the business model, and it is not enough to discover irregularities in financial statements. Good accounting short stories are also able to establish problems that the company is trying to cover up with financial shenanigans.

For example, when Jim Chanos looked at Enron's 1999 10-K filing, his firm found that Enron generated 7 percent return on capital (below its cost of capital) and aggressively used gain-on-sale accounting practices to artificially boost profits. Chanos found Enron's expansion in telecom to be a key mistake. He was also bearish on the telecom sector based on the glut of capacity developing in the sector, and Enron seemed oblivious to this when they announced their telecom initiatives. This belief, coupled with heavy insider selling (an example of insider selling as a leading indicator for a short idea), added conviction to his bearish view on Enron.

Company Events: Earnings, Investor Meetings, and Conferences

Markets closely watch scheduled company events, such as quarterly earnings announcements, investor meetings, management interviews, and industry conferences. The most closely watched events are quarterly earnings announcements, where companies release financial statements, forward guidance and outlook, profit warnings, and status on key initiatives, and management answers questions from analysts during earnings conference calls.

The SEC adopted Regulation FD in 2000 to prevent selective disclosure of material nonpublic information (information that would most certainly impact the stock price) by publicly traded companies. In other words, companies cannot provide sensitive information to a select group of investors ahead of the general public. Consequently, companies are mandated to release such information via press releases or public events, such as scheduled earnings calls. Companies enter a quiet period before such events; their management declines to discuss earnings-related topics and other material information during this time.

The most widely watched numbers in an earnings release are revenue and EPS. Markets can instantly vote down the stock if these numbers do not meet consensus expectations (median of Wall Street analysts' estimates). In other cases, companies may meet or beat these expectations, but their stocks would still fall if the company's forward guidance falls short of expectations or if it issues profit warnings. It is important to estimate revenue, earnings, and other key metrics and compare them with market expectations ahead of earnings.

Companies typically release certain industry-specific metrics only in earnings releases, which are closely watched by the markets as well. Some of the most commonly watched industry-specific metrics include available seat miles and load factors for airlines, book-to-bill ratio and capacity utilization for industrials and materials, comparable store sales for retailers, net interest margin and non-performing assets for banks, and subscriber growth for media and software companies. Chapter 4 provides a list of commonly watched metrics for each industry.

Companies also tend to announce major product launches, restructuring initiatives, and key strategies during annual or special investor meetings. These events build up expectations in the market, and stocks tend to fall when management fails to meet these expectations. Management changes at troubled companies can sometimes lead to good short candidates, especially when they are struggling with an industry slump, daunting competitors, poor acquisitions, or other specific issues. Investor meeting events for troubled companies are especially important as they give management a platform to clearly lay out their turnaround strategy.

When Meg Whitman, HP's CEO, announced in the 2012 investor meeting that HP would not be able to recover and grow for another two years, the stock fell 8 percent on the news. Earlier, as CEO of eBay, Whitman had overseen a successful IPO of the firm and revenue growth for 10 years, from $4 million in 1998 to $8 billion in 2008. She was brought in as CEO to turn around HP.

HP had been struggling since ousting Mark Hurd, its star CEO, in 2010, and had subsequently fired Leo Apotheker, the incoming CEO, in 2011. Apotheker had failed to gain investor confidence amid declining PC demand and was criticized for his acquisition of Palm and Autonomy. The market had laid hopes in Meg Whitman to announce plans to turn around HP sooner than 2014, so her investor meeting was not well received.

These scheduled company events are critical catalysts for short sellers as they digest new information and look for important cues that can impact their short thesis. When a stock has high short interest (heavily shorted), even minor positive news at such events can force a mass exit of short sellers and a massive surge in the stock price.

Some industry sectors release important metrics more frequently, on a weekly or monthly basis. Retailers and automakers announce sales-related data on a monthly basis. Companies can also announce postlaunch sales numbers after important product launches. These data releases are closely watched catalysts that impact stock prices.

Company Events: M&A That Kicks Issues Down the Road

M&A can be a core part of the business model for large companies, such as Johnson & Johnson, Google, and VF Corporation; their corporate development teams constantly hunt for targets that can bring synergy and growth. However, companies can run into integration issues when they make transformative or large acquisitions, especially when they do not have good M&A history. In general, M&A announcements merit close examination when they appear to mask slowing growth and significant business issues.

CASE STUDY:
HMS HOLDINGS (HMSY)

HMS Holdings verifies Medicaid benefit eligibility and audits health care claims to ensure proper payment for services provided by hospitals and other health care entities. State Medicaid programs accounted for 70 percent of its revenues. HMS shares were up about 27 percent after the Supreme Court upheld the Affordable

Care Act in June 2012. Bulls saw the ruling as a boon for HMS because it stood to benefit from increased Medicaid spending.

HMS had acquired Health Data Insights (HDI) for $368 million in December 2011. HMS's slowing core growth was overshadowed by significant new revenues from HDI's recovery audit contractors (RACs) service, and Wall Street was willing to ignore the slowing growth. Research and discussions with industry sources suggested that Medicare RAC revenue could slow down or even decline.

Hospitals had responded aggressively to Medicare RAC audits by appealing an increasing number of denials, especially from HMS, and were winning their appeals and recovering lost revenues. They took their complaints about aggressive RACs to Congress and to the courts to attempt to change or clarify Medicare regulations to preclude incorrect payments due to vague reimbursement rules.

Wall Street was overly optimistic about revenue growth from HMS's rollout of Medicaid RACs. Its research suggested that improper payments to fee-for-service providers accounted for only half of the errors in Medicaid payments as compared with nearly all of the Medicare payment errors. Medicaid RAC programs were also likely to be much less profitable than the Medicare RAC programs because contingency fees were capped at 12.5 percent.

HMS lowered its revenue and earnings guidance on October 4, 2012, amid ongoing issues with its Medicaid program. HMS shares fell approximately 14 percent on the news. Three weeks later, HMS reported third-quarter earnings that missed Wall Street's expectations of revenue and earnings on higher operating costs, causing HMS stock to plunge approximately 24 percent below the target price of $23.

Source: Off Wall Street.

Company Events: Expensive Acquisitions

The acquiring company can rely on cash, stock, debt, or a combination to finance an M&A transaction. The nature of financing provides critical insight into management's view of their own stock valuation. In general, management does not use company stock to make acquisitions if they believe that their stock is undervalued. In such a case, it would make more sense for them to use cash or cheap debt (or a combination of cash and debt) to finance the transaction.

Conversely, management can make liberal use of their stocks to make acquisitions if they believe that their stock is overvalued. All stock M&A deals tend to pick up during the peak bull market cycles. The technology boom of the 1990s probably saw the largest share of such transactions. The two largest and most notable transactions were the $183 billion all-share merger of Vodafone AirTouch and Mannesmann and the $111 billion share and debt merger of AOL and Time Warner. Both transactions failed and have become the subject of business school case studies.

CASE STUDY:
FACEBOOK (FB)

Facebook had raised approximately $1.5 billion over its seven years as a private company from a host of small and large investors, such as Peter Theil, Microsoft, Goldman Sachs, and Digital Sky Technologies. As Facebook decided to reincarnate as a public company, it reported a cash balance of $3.8 billion and, more importantly, cash flow from operations of $1.5 billion in 2011.

Facebook offered 484 million shares in a rollercoaster IPO at $38 per share, raising a total of $18.4 billion; however, approximately $7 billion went to the Facebook coffers, and the rest went to selling stockholders in Facebook. Facebook's cash balance as of May 18, 2012 stood at approximately $11 billion. Facebook' stock was cut to half in its first year as a public company; however, its cash balance was nearly unchanged during this period. During this period, Facebook spent approximately $1 billion on buying servers, storage, and building data centers, while it spent $500 million on buying other companies and patents, including $300 million toward the $1 billion cash and stock acquisition of Instagram in September 2012.

Facebook regained its lost love with Wall Street when it announced that it had made $881 million from news feed advertising revenues in the quarter ending September 2013—$576 million more than the previous quarter. Wall Street was awed by this announcement, and it declared that Facebook was now a mobile company. Shortly after this quarterly report, Facebook was speculated to have offered $3 billion in cash for Snapchat; however, Snapchat turned it down.

Facebook was now trading well above its IPO price by this time. The company made a secondary offering of 27 million shares at $55 per share on December 19, 2013, raising approximately an additional $1.5 billion. Companies usually make secondary offerings when they are strapped for cash or when they want to capitalize on market euphoria or high stock prices. It was too early to tell if Facebook wanted to capitalize on high stock prices.

After the secondary offering, Facebook had raised about $10 billion of outside capital since its inception as a private company. Facebook generated more than $4 billion in cash flows from operations in 2013; its biggest annual use of cash so far had been approximately $2 billion on hardware and data centers, followed by approximately $1.5 billion on research and development. Facebook's cash balance at the end of 2013 stayed unchanged at approximately $11 billion, and they really did not seem to need cash. The reason behind their secondary offering was not very clear.

Within two months of the secondary offering, Facebook announced that it would buy WhatsApp on February 19, 2014, for $19 billion ($4 billion in cash, $12 billion in stock, and $3 billion in restricted stock units). The deal produced sticker shock, and it clearly came at the expense of existing shareholders. With 450 million users at a fee of $1 per year of service, WhatsApp was probably generating $300–400 million in cash revenues. Although the $4 billion cash portion of the deal would dent Facebook's cash war chest, it did not create a hole or impair its ability to make further deals. However, it was a different question whether the $15 billion stock dilution would result in outsized returns for Facebook shareholders. Facebook was treating its stock like paper, creating a tactical shorting opportunity. Facebook stock fell more than 20 percent over the next month, chipping off nearly $38 billion from the market cap—twice the size of the WhatsApp acquisition.

Facebook successfully renovated its business model with mobile advertising revenues, its foray into television advertising, and video advertisements (although the market is largely controlled by YouTube for now). However, the Instagram and WhatsApp acquisitions signal Facebook's strategy to overspend on acquisitions for user experience innovation. Although Facebook has so far been clever in preserving cash in these transactions, its willingness to buy them at any cost signals that Facebook may overpay for future acquisitions. Why is it important to pay attention to the cost of these transactions? Let us compare Facebook's business model with that of Google for some perspective on current Facebook valuation.

There are nearly 2 billion desktops connected to the Internet, compared with a smartphone installed base of 1.7 billion. Google has 80 percent market share in desktop advertising, with an adjusted revenue of $55 billion, whereas Facebook generates nearly $12 billion on an annualized basis. Neither of the companies are available in China. At Facebook's market cap of $200 billion in July 2014, the market believes that Facebook is the Google of mobile advertising. Why?

If we assume that mobile advertising grows more than four times in next four years to $48 billion, the mobile advertising market would become nearly as big as the desktop advertising market. Assume that Facebook captures the entire market in these four years compared to Google, which took seven years to grow from $12 billion to $48 billion. At this point, if Facebook gets a slightly higher multiple of 6× EV/sales versus 5.5× for Google, it will be worth $288 billion—or 48 percent higher—at $112 per share. If we discount the share price back by four years, stock is worth approximately $76 per share, where it is currently trading.

Is Facebook stock priced for perfection? Is there room for speed bumps on Facebook's growth trajectory—for poor acquisitions or expensive acquisitions? Only time will tell.

Macroeconomic Events: Federal Reserve Meetings, Crude Oil Inventory, and More

The Federal Reserve System (the "Fed" or central bank) gets an early look into economic data from its twelve regional banks and responds to data trends through monetary policies of targeting interest rates and money supply. Press releases from periodic Fed meetings provide a glimpse into the state of the economy and the Fed's policy stance. Fiscal policies and trade balances have a direct impact on economic cycles as well.

In addition, other agencies release periodic data to take the pulse of the economy. These leading, coincident, and lagging indicators can have an impact on the overall market or specific industry sectors. For example, a buildup in oil and natural gas inventory can lead to a sell-off in oil stocks; conversely, a decline in inventory can lead to a sell-off in airlines, refineries, and utilities. The most closely watched indicators include unemployment claims and rate, gross domestic product, Michigan consumer sentiment, crude oil inventory, Case-Shiller index, producer price index (PPI), and consumer price index (CPI).

Economic data and policies have a direct impact on the prices of financial assets as well, and the impact is especially pronounced during economic turbulence. Steep market corrections during the financial crisis of 2008, the technology bust of 2000, the Asian crisis of 1997, the savings and loan crisis of the early 1990s, the crash of 1987, the energy crises in 1973 and 1979, the Great Depression of the 1930s, and the banking panic of 1907 are the most prominent in the history of U.S. stock markets.

It is nearly impossible to predict events that trigger a mass exodus from financial assets, such as the Lehman bankruptcy, a Russian default, or a Middle East crisis. However, investors gauge market fear leading up to the crises and during each crisis through several risk indicators, such as the Treasury–Eurodollar spread (figure 1.4), Chicago Board Options Exchange Market Volatility Index, Credit Default Swap Index, Sovereign Credit Default Swap, Term Structure, and Treasury auctions.

Bear markets may seem like a short seller's paradise; however, short sale restrictions, regulations, and vicious bear market rallies can complicate shorting. Modeling economic downturns to find shorts is a different game than modeling company financials

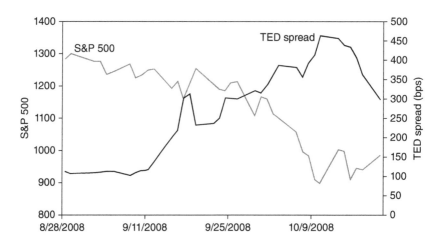

FIGURE 1.4 TED Spread vs. S&P 500 negative correlation during 2008 financial crisis. *Source:* Federal Reserve, S&P Dow Jones Indices.

and is beyond the scope of this book. I have discussed the common characteristics of past crises, the impact of monetary policies, and key economic indicators (in chapter 5), which can signal a tightening credit cycle or recession. Analysts can pick clues from such indicators to identify companies whose business models are more vulnerable to tightening cycles and recession and focus their analysis on related industry sectors.

Recap

- There are three broad short categories: (1) structural shorts with a one- to two-year outlook, (2) tactical shorts with a one-week to one-quarter outlook, and (3) pair trades.
- Structural shorts are longer-term shorts on companies with structural issues with their business or business model. Tactical shorts focus on shorter-term issues and rely on scuttlebutt, surveys, and channel checks.

- Shorting expensive stocks based only on valuation is dangerous.
- There are seven key aspects to analyze in fundamental research: industry, product, financial statements analysis and valuation, customers, management team and incentives, business cycle, and risks.
- When sourcing short ideas, look for signs of business model issues (issues with key client, product, etc.), unsustainable operating or financial leverage, value traps, financial statement issues, and tactical issues.
- Key catalysts that can drive stocks down include investigations, investor announcements, loss of key client or product, product issues, industry slowdown, accounting issues, company events, and macroeconomic issues.

2

Leveraged Businesses
The Upside and Downside

The pound of flesh which I demand of him is dearly bought.
'Tis mine and I will have it.
— SHYLOCK, *MERCHANT OF VENICE*

THIS SCENE FROM SHAKESPEARE'S CLASSIC *Merchant of Venice* is a
crude analogy to demands from creditors when companies breach
their credit agreements, especially when companies become insolvent. Creditors are ahead of stockholders in the queue to stake a
claim when a company fails on its indenture (loan contract). In the
event of a liquidation sale, shareholders may end up getting nothing and creditors can claim everything. The downside for shareholders of heavily indebted companies can be disastrous; they need
to pay careful attention to indentures and whether the debtor company can continue to meet the demands of their credit agreement.

Common Reasons that Companies Borrow

Companies borrow money to finance assets, for short-term working capital (payment to vendors, employees, etc.), or for investment
in long-term fixed assets (plants, real estate, etc.). The related debt
is reported on balance sheets.

In some cases, companies enter into commitments or contracts that might require payments over a long period of time
(e.g., 10-year rent contract) or assume the liabilities (implicit or
explicit) for special-purpose entities related to their businesses.
While such commitments or contracts are similar to borrowed
money, companies may not be obligated to report them as debt
on their balance sheet.

Creditors Versus Shareholders

Creditors and shareholders reside on the liabilities side of the balance sheet. Creditors mostly have the first right to companies'
assets and get preference over stockholders in the event of restructuring, bankruptcy, or liquidation. In other words, when companies are forced to sell assets during liquidation or bankruptcy, they
must repay their creditors before shareholders.

If the company has nothing left after repaying the creditors, its shareholders will be wiped out; that is, the share price
goes to zero. The priority of repayment among creditors is typically in the following order: senior secured creditors (lienhold-
ers on company assets), unsecured creditors, junior creditors,
preferred stockholders, suppliers, employees, and common
shareholders.

Creditors and shareholders effectively own and control company assets, and their ownership stake appears on the liabilities
side of the balance sheet. Because the balance sheet must always
balance, a decline in the value of an asset must be offset by an
increase in the value of other assets or a decrease in shareholder
equity.

However, if the value of overall assets declines and the company faces declining profits or losses, the company may be forced
to take a range of corrective steps such as cutting dividends or
raising additional capital in the form of debt, stock, or preferred

Table 2.1
Eastman Kodak's balance sheet (December 30, 2011)

Assets		Liabilities	
Cash	$861 million	Current	$2150 million
Other current	$1866 million	Long-term debt	$1363 million
Property plan equipment	$895 million	Other	$3288 million
Other	$1056 million	Shareholder equity	$2352 million
Total assets	$4678 million	Total liabilities	$4678 million

Source: Eastman Kodak SEC filings, 2011 annual report.

investments. Such actions dilute the existing shareholder value, which may even be wiped out in the extreme event of bankruptcy or liquidation.

Let us take a look at Eastman Kodak's balance sheet before they filed for bankruptcy on January 19, 2012. In table 2.1, we find that Kodak's total liabilities ($3.288 billion + $1.363 billion + $2.15 billion) were more than total assets ($4.678 billion), implying negative equity. Equity would have continued to suffer if Kodak had continued to post losses or dispose assets for a loss.[1]

Takeaway
Companies borrow to finance assets, working capital, and expansion plans. Creditors are ahead of shareholders to get repaid during distress. Shareholders can get wiped out in the event of a bankruptcy.

Financial Leverage Versus Operating Leverage

Financial leverage, or gearing, measures the degree of indebtedness of a company resulting from interest-bearing loans. The most common leverage ratios are debt to equity; debt to earnings before interest, taxes, depreciation, and amortization (EBITDA); and earnings before interest (EBIT) to interest. Companies report short-term and long-term liabilities on their balance sheets. These liabilities can arise from borrowing needs (as mentioned previously) or from other liabilities such as pension liabilities, unpaid claims, and so on.

Operating leverage results from the high fixed costs required to run a business, such as the costs to run a manufacturing plant, pay employees, or rent storefronts. The most common operating leverage ratio is percent change in operating profit to percent change in sales. Companies report these fixed costs either as operating expenses (salaries, rents, etc.) in the income statement or as fixed assets (i.e., property, plant, and equipment) in the balance sheet.

Leverage can lead to additional revenues and possibly greater profits for stockholders. Because stockholders do not need to invest any extra money to earn these additional profits, added leverage boosts their returns or upside when the business is doing well. However, if the business, industry, or economy takes a wrong turn, leverage can lead to an equally disastrous downside. Excessive leverage behaves like a ticking time bomb during troubled times if companies are unable to service their debt.

Off-Balance Sheet Items: Commitments, Contingencies, and Special-Purpose Vehicles

Not all liabilities are reported as debt on the balance sheet. Accounting rules and treatments of certain debt or leverage-like transactions allow companies to report liabilities as off-balance sheet items. For example, lease treatment rules for operating assets allow companies to report them as off-balance sheet items in special notes, unlike capital assets.

Companies may enter into other forms of commitment, such as purchase commitments with their suppliers, capital commitments to purchase assets or decommission plants, construction commitments, third-party guarantees, and licensing agreements. We cannot get an accurate picture of liabilities without including such commitments because these items are reported separately, outside the balance sheet.

Contingent liabilities and claims may arise due to the occurrence of specific external events such as legal, patent, tax, regulatory, environmental, or pension-related claims. Such liabilities may also arise from other future events that lead to payment obligations for the company, such as claims related to product warranty, a line of credit tapped by a bank customer, or liabilities arising from derivative commitments.

Special-purpose entities (SPEs) and special-purpose vehicles (SPVs) became infamous during the Enron scandal when Enron set up SPVs and entered into bogus transactions with them to generate fake revenues. SPVs can either be set up as subsidiaries of the parent company or as independent companies to hold assets. Creditors of the parent company cannot lay their claims on these assets in the event of a bankruptcy. SPVs are common among financial services companies and banks.

During the subprime lending boom, banks had set up SPVs, such as structured collateralized debt obligations, structured investment vehicles (SIVs), and other investment conduits, to buy the inventory of subprime loans and structured products that were financed largely by short-term wholesale loans. In theory, banks were not liable if the value of assets bought by these SPVs dropped; the lenders to these SPVs were on the hook for losses. So, why should we have paid attention to these SPVs?

In 2007, HSBC took the high road to bring the SIVs onto its own balance sheet and Citigroup followed suit. HSBC maintained that its earnings would not be materially impacted by this bailout. However, both HSBC and Citigroup were forced to take massive write-downs as credit conditions deteriorated.

Leverage Thrills but Kills

Leverage is a double-edged sword. When sales are growing at a company with high operating or financial leverage, its operating profit can grow even faster. When a company's business model fails, growth falters, or sales decline, leverage can magnify its losses. The balance sheet does not balance when these losses flow from income statement to balance sheet, forcing shareholder equity to absorb the losses. A streak of losses can even wipe out shareholder equity.

Takeaway
Financial leverage increases with borrowings, while operating leverage increases with fixed costs. Both can accelerate profits as well as losses. Leverage can be hidden in commitments and contingent liabilities.

Companies can have both financial leverage and operating leverage. Let us take a closer look at some leveraged businesses. I will begin with a short thesis on Office Depot that I published in 2010. I have highlighted the key parts of my analysis of this company's stock.

CASE STUDY:
OFFICE DEPOT (ODP)

In June 2009, Office Depot received a $350 million convertible preferred investment from BC Partners, giving the private equity firm up to a 20 percent stake in Office Depot. Sales at Office Depot had been slumping by more than 10 percent for two consecutive years amid the recession and a challenged office supplies retailing market. This investment had eased liquidity concerns. However, nine months later, Office Depot's sales continued to slide in the face of increased competition and tough economic conditions.

In February 2010, CNN Money reported on a U.S. Securities and Exchange Commission (SEC) investigation that was in the final stages of settlement and a fresh probe into whether Office Depot overcharged its government customers. I became interested in Office Depot and started going through their public filings.[2] I stumbled upon several indicators of downside risk unrelated to the investigation. There seemed a high likelihood for some of the risks to materialize soon.

Balance Sheet

The $660 million debt on balance sheet or debt-to-equity (D/E) ratio of 0.85 did not reflect the company's true leverage. After making an adjustment for a $1.25 billion off-balance sheet revolver and $2.16 billion of capitalized leases, the D/E increased significantly to 6 ($2.16 billion of capitalized lease based on $270 million of operating leases and approximately 8x rent; 40 percent of Office Depot lease terms were more than 5 years).

With a fixed coverage ratio close to 1, continuing negative free cash flow, and operating profits, Office Depot seemed to risk breaching its credit covenants and entering the zone of insolvency. Office Depot had both financial and operating leverage.

Profitability

Office Depot's return to profitability was not only a function of how aggressively the company formed a restructuring plan but also of the improvement in economic conditions, a lower unemployment rate, and rational price competition by competitors. Office Depot earned an average of 10 percent return on invested capital (ROIC) between 2000 and 2007; however, the company continued to face lower operating margins and higher debt costs over the next two years, which lowered its likelihood to return to mid-single-digit ROIC.

Office Depot also renewed its government contracts in the first quarter of 2010. The company's pricing was expected to suffer from the budget constraint of state governments, especially California.

Shareholder Dilution and Dividends

In October 2009, Office Depot requested shareholder approval for conversion and voting rights for BC Partners' preferred shares. The preferred convertibles had a strike price of $5, and ODP shares were trading at ~$8. Convertibles were deep in the money with a high likelihood of conversion that could dilute the current shares by 76 million (more than 20 percent).

Office Depot had never declared or paid cash dividends on common stock, and its asset-based credit facility limited payment of dividends based on its current fixed charge ratio threshold. Office Depot paid preferred dividends in the form of pay-in-kind notes.

Lack of Management Incentives

Management employment contracts were revised after the October shareholder vote to trigger a change in control and enhanced severance benefits of $11.3 million to the chief executive officer (CEO) and a combined $6 million to two other key executives. Under the new contract, Steve Odland (CEO) was eligible for a $5 million retainer, which vested over the next three years. Under the revised contract, Odland was also entitled to a cash severance payment of two times his base salary and a bonus of no less than $5.2 million.

Similar golden parachute agreements with other executives signaled misaligned incentives for management, as the executives were completely protected in the event that the shareholders' returns suffered. The criteria for the performance goals of management were not clearly laid out and depended on earnings per share (EPS), net earnings, net operating profit after tax, return on equity, comparable store sales, etc., or a combination of these factors; also, these goals were subject to arbitrary adjustments by the company board. The management did not seem to be accountable for a swift turnaround of the company.

Competition and Struggling Industry

The U.S. office supplies industry totals approximately $300 billion, with $170 billion in retail sales and $130 billion in contract sales. It is a highly fragmented industry, with the top three retailers— Staples, Office Depot, and OfficeMax—having a combined 10.6 percent and 12.3 percent market share in office retail and contract solutions, respectively. Through the financial crisis, Staples opened stores in geographies where Office Depot and OfficeMax struggled; however, comparable store sales for all three retailers declined during this period (figure 2.1).

The remaining market was shared by large warehouses, merchandisers, and superstores, as well as smaller and niche local office suppliers and internet retailers. Amazon, Sam's Club, Costco

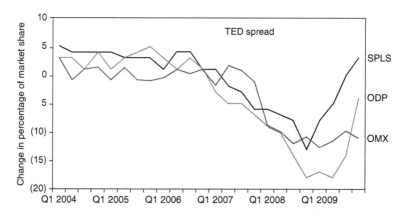

FIGURE 2.1 Staples, Office Depot, Office Max same store sales 2004–2010.
Source: Company SEC filings.

and a few other low-cost competitors entered the office supplies business in 2009, elevating concerns on pricing in an already price-sensitive industry.

Top Shareholders (as of March 2010)

In an 8-K filing, ODP announced, "On October 14, 2009, Office Depot shareholders overwhelmingly approved the conversion, at the option of the holders of our Series A and Series B Preferred stock (BC Partners), into shares of common stock." It is important to note that BC Partners is not listed as a shareholder in table 2.2 because they had not yet exercised their conversion option.

Valuation

At 20× consensus of the 2012 estimated earnings, Office Depot seemed to price the best case scenario of 10 percent sales growth over the next two years. In that case, Office Depot could earn diluted $0.4 per share after BC Partners' conversion. At $8 per share, the stock was priced for perfection (tables 2.3 through 2.5).

Table 2.2
Office Depot's top shareholders

Holder name	Position	Position change	Market value	Percent out
Alliance Bernstein LP	38,712,949	28,055,555	308,155,074	14.09
Ziff Bros. Investments LLC	22,622,844	(2,144,539)	180,077,838	8.23
State Street Global Advisors	14,897,049	4,444,991	118,580,510	5.42
Vanguard Group, Inc.	14,557,366	220,037	115,876,633	5.30

Source: ODP SEC filings.

Table 2.3
Office Depot's earning sensitivity to sales and EBITDA growth

Earnings per share - (EPS in the grid)		Sales growth (right axis)						
EBITDA (left axis)		–2%	0%	2%	6%	8%	10%	11%
	0.5%	(0.4)	(0.4)	(0.4)	(0.3)	(0.3)	(0.3)	(0.3)
	1.0%	(0.2)	(0.2)	(0.2)	(0.2)	(0.2)	(0.2)	(0.2)
	1.5%	(0.1)	(0.1)	(0.1)	(0.1)	(0.1)	(0.1)	(0.1)
	2.0%	0.0	0.0	0.0	0.1	0.1	0.1	0.1
	2.5%	0.2	0.2	0.2	0.2	0.2	0.2	0.2
	3.0%	0.3	0.3	0.3	0.3	0.4	0.4	0.4
	3.5%	0.4	0.4	0.4	0.5	0.5	0.5	0.5

Source: Artham Capital Partners LLC.

Table 2.4
Sensitivity analysis: Impact of sales and EBITDA growth on EPS

Capital structure/leverage		Valuation/consensus	
Debt/equity	37%	P/E LTM NA	
(Debt + Cap Lease)/EBITDAR	6.74	Consensus 2 buy/2 sells/11 holds	
Debt/EBITDA	3.6	EPS 10	
EBITDAR/(Interest + Rent)	P/E 10e	NA	
S&P Rating	B (Stable)	EPS 11e 0.2	
P/B	2.8	P/E 11e 40.7	
EV/EBITDA	10.65	P/E 12e 19.1	

NA, not available.

Table 2.5
Key financial data for Office Depot (as of March 13, 2010)

Stock data/balance sheet		Income statement operating performance		Returns	
Stock price	$8	Rev (mm) LTM	$12.14 billion	Div Yield	0%
Market cap	$2.2 billion	EBITDA (mm) LTM	$200.3 million	ROE (LTM)	−52%
Shares out (float %)	273.42 million (98%)	EBITDAR (mm) LTM	$498.6 million	ROE (00–07)	10%
Enterprise value	$2.26 billion	EBIT (mm) LTM	(23) million	ROA (LTM)	−12%
52-Week range	$1.02–8.30	Comp store sales LTM	−14%	ROA (00–07)	5%
Short percent of float	10.30%	Comp store sales/last 3-year average	−11%	ROIC (LTM)	−24%
Short ratio	5	EPS ($/sh.) LTM	(2.30)	ROIC (00–07)	11%

Source: ODP SEC filings.

Risks to My Short Thesis

This thesis is not without risk. First-quarter earnings are seasonally strongest for Office Depot, and the stock typically rose after the first-quarter earnings release. Also, office supplies sales are negatively correlated to levels of unemployment, so an improvement in unemployment numbers could drive the stock up. Lastly, Office Depot had a high short interest ratio of 10 percent, which could result in significant stock price volatility due to a short squeeze.*

---

*See the Glossary for a definition of *short squeeze*.

How Did Office Depot Play Out?

Office Depot was scheduled to report earnings on April 27, 2010, a month after I published the report. On April 26, 2010, a bulge bracket analyst upgraded Office Depot to neutral, citing channel checks indicating that the company was slowly getting over the disruptions from poor integration from a prior acquisition. The stock rose 10 percent on the upgrade. I was blindsided by the analyst upgrade, especially because the upgrade happened one day before the earnings announcement. Interestingly, the risk section of the analyst upgrade report pointed to some of the issues I had raised about Office Depot. I remained bearish. On April 27, 2010, Office Depot announced earnings that missed street expectations. The stock fell 21 percent that day and continued to fall to near half of its value over the next six months.

Takeaway
It is hard to find shorts with as many negative catalysts as Office Depot: losing market share, structural issues with business model, high debt levels, share dilution, and poorly aligned management incentives.

CASE STUDY:
SOUTHWEST AIRLINES (LUV)

Airline stocks had fallen 20 to 60 percent in 2008 amid rising oil prices. Southwest Airlines was an exception, up over 10 percent in 2008, because it had hedged half of its fuel needs for 2008 and 2009. Southwest was a better airline operator that steered away from the traditional hub-and-spoke airline model to a point-to-point flight model geared toward shorter-distance travelers. Southwest had better debt service ratios, with a debt-to-EBITDA ratio of ~2.0 versus ~5 for most other airlines, including American, Continental, US Airways, and others. Most airlines had announced capacity cuts, but Southwest planned to buy 14 additional planes in 2008, expecting an ROIC of more than 15 percent on new planes. However, Southwest's cost model was no different from other airlines (table 2.6).

The cost model for the capital-intensive airlines industry is marked by high operating leverage from salary expenses, fuel costs, and landing and maintenance fees. Fuel and wages constitute 50 to 70 percent of revenues. Airlines have little control over costs

Table 2.6
Comparative statistics for airlines in the first quarter of 2008

	LUV	NWA	AMR	CAL	LCC	DAL
Fuel expense (million $)	753	1,114	2,050	1,262	955	1,422
Average cost of fuel ($/gallon)	2.01	2.65	2.73	2.80	2.88	2.85
Fuel used (million gallons)	373	420	680	451	286	500
Passengers carried (millions)	21.5	15.9	NA	16.4	NA	NA
Revenue miles (millions)	17,592	19,214	34,630	22,280	14,489	28,205
Revenue yield per revenue passenger miles	13.72	13.78	14.32	14.47	13.48	14.54
Available seat miles (millions)	25,193	23,359	44,158	28,376	18,335	36,092
Load factor (%)	69.8	82.3	78.4	78.5	79.0	78.1

Source: SEC filings.
NA, not available.

and a limited ability to pass along cost inflation to passenger fares. Financial leverage resulting from fixed obligations, such as aircraft leasing and airport property financing, adds interest costs to the operating expenses. The inherent leverage in airline business models makes these companies more susceptible to failure during economic downturns or oil price crises. The industry saw hundreds of bankruptcies since 1990 triggered by an airline's default on interest payments.

Although Southwest would most likely survive the ongoing oil crisis due to its fuel hedge program (table 2.7), its earnings would suffer once the hedge program stepped down from 70 percent of fuel needs in 2008 to 55 percent in 2009 and 30 percent in 2010. Southwest had reported the value of its hedge to be worth $5 billion; the value would be closer to $6.5 billion if jet fuel prices continued to remain high at ~$3 per gallon through 2012.

Table 2.7
Southwest's 5-year fuel hedge program

	2008	2009	2010	2011	2012
Fuel need (millions of gallons)	1,500	1,590	1,685	1,787	1,894
Hedged (millions of gallons)	789	875	506	268	284
Hedged (millions of barrels)	25	28	16	9	9
Average crude price ($/barrel)	51	51	63	64	63
Value of hedge (millions of $)	2,265	2,511	1,256	657	706
Net present value (NPV in millions of $)	6,561				

Source: Southwest SEC filings.

However, if crude oil and jet fuel prices stayed so unprecedentedly high, Southwest's EBITDA would likely fall by half and result in losses by 2009. Fuel prices would need to fall by at least 33 percent in order for Southwest to maintain its EBITDA margins; however, the value of its hedge program would be cut by half to ~$3 billion (more than 30 percent of Southwest's market cap). Therefore, Southwest would have lost money whether fuel prices went up or down.

Fuel costs seemed to be a negative for the stock, as did airline demand. The International Air Transport Association (IATA) reported in a May 2008 press release that slowdown in airline demand growth continued on the heels of the sharp downward trend that began in December 2007, and the airline industry had begun to feel the impact of the U.S. credit crunch. In a subsequent press release in the same month, IATA said, "North American carriers recorded 3.8 percent demand growth in international passenger traffic as capacity continued to shift to international markets. This was outstripped by capacity expansion of 6.2 percent."[3]

There were signs of cyclical downturn in the airline industry. Recent attempts by American Airlines and United to increase fares were met with a decline in passenger demand. Southwest traffic had showed signs of slowdown with a 0.7 percent increase in June, a seasonally strong month, despite a 5.7 percent increase in capacity. Historically, summer had been a strong season for airlines, especially Southwest, which had historically reported strong second-quarter results.

Southwest's enterprise value was ~$12.2 billion and the stock seemed overvalued, trading between 14x and 15x the estimated EBITDA for 2009, given the current demand outlook and high oil prices. The upside risk for shorting Southwest Airlines seemed limited as compared to other airline stocks, which had fallen by over 50 percent and were more likely to surge if crude prices fell.

I recommended shorting the stock after the company reported second-quarter earnings results on July 28, 2008. My short thesis was not without risks, including a possible consolidation wave in the airline industry, Southwest's $500 million stock repurchase, a possible return in airline demand, Southwest's change in expansion plans, or shelving expansion plans altogether. The last risk seemed unlikely because 45 percent of its fleet was older than 17 years.

How Did Southwest Airlines Play Out?

Southwest Airlines posted a strong second quarter as I expected, and the stock rose 5 percent to close at $15.76 on July 29. However, airline demand kept falling as IATA reported a continued decline in August and an alarming drop in September. Oil prices sold off 30 percent from July highs after the Federal Reserve chairman said that high oil prices had caused significant demand destruction within the United States. Southwest's hedge lost value amid falling oil prices, leading them to post the first loss in 17 years in the third quarter of 2008. Lehman Brothers filed for bankruptcy on September 15, 2008, leading to a severe credit crunch and the longest recession since the Great Depression of 1929. Southwest stock fell sharply with the rest of the airline stocks in the ensuing macroeconomic slowdown.

Takeaway

Airlines have high operating leverage, which accentuates the impact of economic downturns. High fuel costs and legacy union issues have marred airlines from time to time and even led to bankruptcies.

CASE STUDY:
CIENA CORPORATION (CIEN)

Ciena's revenues grew ~15 percent and stock rose 56 percent in 2013 as Ciena benefited from an increase in AT&T's capital expenditures on 40G and 100G network infrastructures. However, Ciena faced some key risks that posed a considerable downside to the stock. AT&T accounted for ~$133 million of incremental revenue (more than 50 percent of its revenue growth in 2013) while accounting for ~17.9 percent of its $2.1 billion revenues in 2013 and 13.5 percent of its $1.8 billion revenues in 2012. Ciena's business model had customer concentration risk.

While Ciena could benefit from upgrades by smaller U.S. carriers as well as international carriers, some of these upgrades were not on the horizon for at least a year. Besides, such upgrades did not have the potential to contribute as much as AT&T or Verizon —two of Ciena's largest clients. Ciena had a good presence in North America but low exposure in China, where it had incurred losses in the past.

Communications network solution vendors compete aggressively, mostly on price. Ciena faced not only well-capitalized competitors (ALU, Huawei, etc.) but also smaller competitors such as Infinera, which were able to make inroads into large carriers such as AT&T (Infinera had become a preferred AT&T vendor). Ciena had barely eked out any EPS in two of the past seven years, despite the fact that that its revenue has nearly quadrupled—a hint of poor margins in this business.

Management incentives were tied to sales targets rather than profitability, which could very well cause the streak of operating losses to continue even when revenues are growing. Ciena's CEO has been running the company since the technology bust, when the stock was trading at $400 per share in May 2001. (The stock had corrected from its peak of $1,000 per share in 2000.) If you looked at the peak sales in the last ten-year cycle, Ciena's sales were always very lumpy. I believed that management would not be able to provide a positive margin outlook at an upcoming analyst meeting on April 3, 2014.

Ciena also had a highly leveraged balance sheet with a history of losses and poor operating cash flow for the last five years. Its convertibles from Nortel acquisition and other convertibles could potentially dilute the stockholders by at least 10 percent. With a debt/EBITDA of 9–10 and poor EBITDA growth, Ciena seemed precariously leveraged with an outstanding convertible obligation of ~$1.2 billion. The company's credit agreements limited its ability to pay cash dividends and repurchase stock, as well as to repay debt in certain cases.

Ciena should have traded at or below an EV/sales of 1, given its high operating and financial leverage, lumpy historical sales, growth, customer concentration, and dilution risk from convertibles. I published a short thesis on March 20, 2014.

How Did Ciena Play Out?

Street analysts were torn into two camps after management provided a dismal operating profit outlook in the analyst meeting on April 3, 2014. The stock fell more than 20 percent over the next few weeks.

Industries with Inherent Dependence on Leverage

Most asset-intensive businesses (banks, miners, utilities, telecom carriers, real estate investment trusts, etc.) are naturally more leveraged than asset-light businesses (e.g., software and services companies). Investment in such businesses requires special attention to the terms of their credit agreements and off-balance sheet commitments, as well as their financial ability to service their debt.

Capital-intensive industries such as shipping, airlines, banks, and miners cannot operate without leverage or external borrowing. This inherent dependence on leverage leads to risk in the business model of weaker players or chronic structural issues for the entire industry during downturn cycles.

Leveraged industries tend to suffer more than other industries during macroeconomic slowdowns. Leveraged industries are also more prone to suffer from capacity or supply glut in their industry or in a competing industry. For example, the shipping industry saw a glut in supply of very large crude carriers and bulk carriers from 2009 to 2010 while global demand for oil dropped. Two of the largest shipping companies filed for bankruptcy in 2011, marking the longest slump in the history of the shipping industry as many other shipping companies filed for bankruptcy protection through 2012.

Similarly, the coal industry suffered from a glut in the U.S. supply of natural gas in 2012. Figure 2.2 shows the impact of the decline of natural gas prices on coal demand after the discovery of

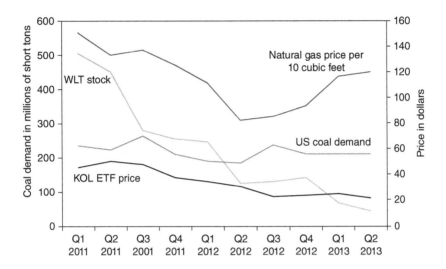

FIGURE 2.2 Impact of decline in natural gas price on coal stocks. *Source:* EIA, WLT SEC Filings, Bloomberg.

vast new supplies of natural gas in U.S. shale deposits. As utilities began to switch to more natural gas for electricity generation, coal prices tanked and coal stocks suffered.

Players with poor operating economics in troubled and leveraged industries tend to have high short interest. It can be extremely painful to short such high beta stocks (stocks can move up violently on a small piece of good news), and regulators may impose short-selling restrictions on them from time to time.

Recap

- Companies borrow to finance assets, working capital, and expansion.
- Creditors are ahead of shareholders to get repaid during distress or downturn. Shareholders can get wiped out in the event of a bankruptcy.

- Financial leverage increases with borrowings, while operating leverage increases with fixed costs. Leverage accelerates profits as well as losses.
- Leverage can be hidden in commitments and contingent liabilities.
- It is important to identify any negative catalysts while researching shorts, such as losing market share, structural issues, high debt levels, issues with share structure, and poorly aligned management incentives.
- Economic downturns or industry-specific issues have an accentuated impact on companies with high operating and financial leverage.
- The financial crisis forced many banks and airlines out of business.
- Leveraged industries are also more prone to suffer from capacity or supply gluts in their industry or in a competing industry.
- Coal stocks suffered as a result of the discovery of natural gas supplies.

3

Structural Issues in Industries

To improve is to change; to be perfect is to change often.
— WINSTON S. CHURCHILL

GREAT COMPANIES RESPOND TO CHANGE; however, changes in the marketplace can sometimes completely alter traditional business models and threaten the viability of once-successful businesses. The rise of the Internet and e-commerce broke the business models for many traditional industries, including newspaper and book publishing, brick-and-mortar retailers, and music and video distributors. Their model needed to change often and keep changing forever. Stocks of declining businesses can appear cheap based on historical performance; however, they can prove to be value traps if the decline continues for an extended period of time. They have no moat around their business.

In other cases, companies can suffer from poor growth prospects, loss in demand for their products, bad investments, and other issues specific to their own business situations. When a fast-growing company shows signs of slowdown, its valuation multiples shrink as the market begins to question the growth story and temper its growth expectations. Technology, consumer, and pharmaceutical sectors tend to contribute the lion's share of growth stories and broken growth stories.

Value traps and broken growth stories can appear cheap for many reasons: cash on their balance sheet, recent peaks in their revenues and profitability, the support of a key customer, trough valuation multiples, and continued expectations for management to deliver good results. The investment case for such companies hinges on the question, "Has the business model changed for the worse and has it changed permanently?" Excess leverage, possible write-downs on inventories or investments, and regulatory requirements can further accentuate issues with the business model. Cheap stocks can get cheaper—dirt cheap—and eventually become worthless.

Takeaway
Companies may suffer significant blows to their business model that may be irreparable. Their growth story may be broken as a result of disruptive products, competition, etc., or the value of their business may be on a structural decline.

Value Traps

Value traps are like fallen-angel stocks, whose glory days may not come back because of structural changes in the business or industry. Let me begin with my experience with value traps in two completely different industries: AIG (a multiline insurer) and Carpetright (the largest carpet retail chain in the United Kingdom).

CASE STUDY:
AMERICAN INSURANCE GROUP (AIG)

In 2007, I joined Swiss Reinsurance in their structured credit group. Our group worked with large investment banks to sell credit default swaps (CDS) on structured credit products and competed with both monoline insurers (e.g., MBIA, Ambac, FSA) and multiline insurers (e.g., AIG). In the summer of 2007, we saw the beginning of a credit crunch and suffered severe losses as the price of credit protection skyrocketed. On November 19, 2007, Swiss Re announced $1.2 billion mark-to-market losses on its $5.3 billion credit investments. Approximately $1 billion of the losses came from a 100 percent write-down of the asset-backed security (ABS)-collateralized debt obligations (CDO) portfolio. These investments were worth zero.

During the six months of this credit crunch, I gained immense insights into the financial sector. I could see that other monoline and multiline insurers would be forced to take similar mark-to-market losses on their subprime-related ABS-CDO investments. As per their August 2007 investor presentation, AIG had $64 billion of notional investments in CDOs with subprime exposure, including $19.4 billion of BBB-rated mezzanine collateral. They also had net exposure to $280+ billion corporate CDS, which was beginning to show signs of distress as well.

Most of these AIG investments were marked to model. In other words, they relied on their own optimistic housing market assumptions to estimate the price of their investments—unlike Swiss Re, which had marked down the prices based on low market prices for similar securities. If AIG were as aggressive in marking its investments as Swiss Re, their losses would be anywhere between $20 billion and $40 billion (15–30 percent of AIG's market cap of $147 billion on December 31, 2007).

However, accounting treatment for these derivative transactions allowed AIG to not report them on its balance sheet. They were disclosed under special notes in AIG's filings. An excerpt from the annual report said, "Notional amount is not a quantification of market risk or credit risk and the hedge is highly effective, while it uses the periodic dollar offset not recorded on the consolidated balance sheet."[1]   AIG was trading at a historically low price-to-book (P/B) multiple of ~1.4 and appeared to be a value stock.

AIG seemed cheap based on its brand strength in traditional multi-line insurance. However, AIG's business model had changed with its foray into these off-balance sheet transactions in securitized products. Insurers like AIG earned a premium of 0.1–0.3 percent for insuring bonds, or 10–30 basis points per $100 of risky credit. In a stress scenario, AIG's leverage from exposure to these products could significantly hurt their shareholders. AIG seemed like a value trap.

Monoline insurers, such as MBIA and Ambac, were in a similar position with even greater leverage of 50 to 100 from exposure to these products. They got the name *monolines* because they operated in one line of business, insuring municipal bonds. Monolines started in the 1970s by insuring municipal bonds which had rarely defaulted in the last 30 years. These insurers had steered away from their core business to insuring risky ABS-CDOs, which were much more likely to default. Securitized products, such as ABS-CDOs, had lower-quality underlying assets such as subprime, alternative A-paper (Alt-A), which did not have a long history of performance. These loans were much more likely to turn sour than municipal bonds and traditional insurance products.

These insurers seemed cheap based on the historical performance of their traditional business, but their risk of losses from significant leverage and the risks associated with their new securitized products business made them value traps. My short thesis on AIG and monolines landed me the analyst job at our long-short equities group in December 2007.

How Did AIG Play Out?

On February 11, 2008, AIG announced a material weakness in its investment portfolio following a dispute with its auditor, PricewaterhouseCoopers (PwC). PwC disagreed with the mark-to-model methodology used to price the company's CDS contracts, forcing AIG to mark down its CDO portfolio. (Selling CDS on the CDOs was tantamount to investing in the CDOs.) The stock fell ~12 percent on the news, but it recovered the losses after two weeks.

AIG released earnings on February 29, 2008, announcing bigger losses on the CDOs. The head of AIG's Financial Products group was fired. The stock fell 10 percent to $46.86 on larger-than-expected losses. Two months later, AIG announced a sale of 196.7 million shares at $38 and other equity and fixed-income securities to raise $20 billion and cover the impact of these losses. The stock was down another 30 percent by the end of May. It seemed that AIG might be able to navigate through tough times after raising this capital, but things got surprisingly tougher for AIG, leading to their eventual bailout by the Federal Reserve ("the Fed") in September 2008.

Takeaway

While AIG seemed cheap on a P/B basis, its book value was inflated because it did not account for off-balance sheet liabilities from the CDS business. Because AIG could suffer losses on this protection well in excess of its book value, it was not a value stock based on cheap P/B.

More on the Financial Crisis to Better Understand the AIG Short Case

An excerpt from the U.S. Department of Housing and Urban Development (HUD) website says, "Typically, subprime loans are for persons with blemished or limited credit histories." Lending to these risky borrowers grew from $40 billion in 1994 to $160 billion in 1999. Subprime lending got a shot in the arm from a new HUD regulation in 2000 that boosted government-sponsored enterprise participation in the subprime market. Subprime lending grew to $330 billion in 2003 as Freddie Mac and Fannie Mae purchased more than 50 percent of all subprime loans.[2]

In 2003, 58 percent of subprime loans were securitized. Origination volumes of Alt-A loans (for borrowers with less than full documentation) began to rise. Subprime lending grew to $600 billion in 2006, with 75 percent of the subprime market financed by private-label residential mortgage-backed securities. Subprime loans then accounted for 20 percent of total mortgage originations, and Alt-A loans accounted for another 13 percent. Low interest rates and poor underwriting standards increased the availability of loans, leading to high home prices and fueling growth in home equity loans (i.e., a second mortgage on the home). Rising home prices and unprecedented growth in subprime, Alt-A, and home equity loans flooded the secondary mortgage market with a slew of securitized products. While higher home prices were good as a collateral value, they deterred new buyers due to lower affordability.

New products, such as adjustable-rate mortgages (ARMs), offered low teaser rates for the first few years; however, rates were designed to increase by 4–6 percent after the reset of this teaser period. Continued deterioration in underwriting standards led to a variety of poor-quality loans, such as "liar loans" and NINJAs (no income, no job, no assets). Investor demand for such loans emboldened investment banks to keep large inventories of subprime loans. The bank stock index KBW Bank Index (BKX) hit an all-time high of $121.06 on February 20, 2007.

Beginning of the Subprime Crisis

New Century, the second-largest subprime lender listed on the New York Stock Exchange, announced on February 7, 2007, that it would restate its earnings and report a loss in the fourth quarter of 2006 due to rising delinquencies on subprime loans. Two months later, they filed for bankruptcy, marking the beginning of the subprime crisis. Soon after, HSBC announced huge losses from its subprime unit in California. The contagion began to spread to secondary mortgage products, such as structured CDOs, SIVs, and other investment conduits. Banks that created and managed SIVs to make investments in secondary mortgage products were forced to consolidate these SIVs on the balance sheet and take massive write-downs. HSBC and

Citigroup were the first victims. Monoline insurers were the next victims, from financial guarantees on super-senior ABS-CDOs.

Government's Initial Response

In late 2007, Treasury Secretary Henry Paulson indicated that the government may not allow resets on ARMs, which could potentially force en masse default on a majority of loans issued in 2004 and 2005. The Fed started cutting rates in 2007 and bailed out Bear Stearns in March 2008 to allay market fears. The Fed opened the discount window—their tool to lend directly to banks during emergency situations—for a period of six months to calm down the markets.

Lehman Bankruptcy and AIG Downgrade

Subprime delinquency rates rose dramatically by the end of 2007. Both fixed-rate and ARM subprime delinquencies rose from 10 percent in 2007 to 20 percent by the summer of 2008. ARM subprime lenders began to reset rates in 2007 and sparked an increase in foreclosures. Foreclosures on homes financed by ARM subprime loans rose from 2 percent in the beginning of 2007 to 7 percent in the summer of 2008.

In July 2008, financial stocks started sinking again, and Freddie Mac and Fannie Mae were the next candidates for bailout. On July 21, the Securities and Exchange Commission placed a one-week ban (later extending it to three weeks) on short selling stocks of seventeen large investment banks, along with Freddie Mac and Fannie Mae. However, financial stocks continued to fall like dominoes, forcing Fannie Mae and Freddie Mac into government conservatorship on September 6, 2008.

In a sharp contrast to its decision to bail out Bear Stearns, the government decided to let Lehman Brothers file for bankruptcy on September 15, 2008. Standard & Poor downgraded AIG by three notches on the same day after its downgrade warning on September 12, 2008. The AIG downgrade triggered at least $13 billion in additional collateral calls on its CDO transactions, and the stock fell 61 percent on the news to $4.76. Two days later, the Fed announced $85 billion in rescue loans to AIG and the U.S. government took a 79.9 percent stake in exchange for the bailout.

This was the beginning of unprecedented intervention by the U.S. Treasury to restore confidence in financial markets and thaw the frozen credit markets. Markets did not reach bottom for the next six months until the Fed essentially backed all new debt issuances and provided cover to many mortgage-backed structured products.

Takeaway
The collapse in the subprime mortgage market permanently changed the business model of the financial services industry and demand for related securitized products collapsed (figure 3.1). Short analysis can often uncover issues that are not only endemic to one company (AIG in this case) but also pervade in the broader industry or economy.

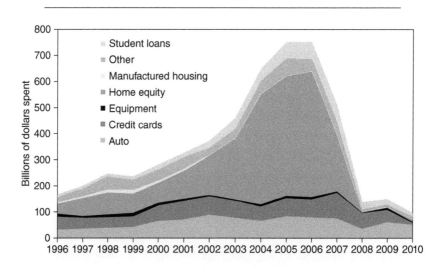

FIGURE 3.1 Securitized ABS product issuances. *Source:* SIFMA.

CASE STUDY:
CARPETRIGHT (LSE: CPR)

The floor covering sector declined with the housing sector after the 2008 financial crisis. Carpetright, the largest U.K. carpet retailer, faced a steep decline in carpet sales, which constituted ~80 percent of their total revenues. Carpetright had navigated the downturn better than its peers, Allied Carpets and Floors 2 Go, which ended up filing for bankruptcy. They enjoyed negative working capital due to their size and scale of operations, paying their suppliers two to three months after making the sale. However, as I researched the stock more, I could see a few traits of a value trap.[3]

At £700 per share in June 2012, Carpetright stock seemed to expect the operating profits to return to precrisis levels based on its enterprise value to earnings before interest and tax valuation of 40; however, carpet margins had declined due to an increase in raw material costs (figure 3.2). Monthly mortgage approvals, a key driver for carpet sales, were at half of their precrisis levels (figure 3.3). Carpetright closed more than fifty stores amid these structural challenges in the carpet industry and entered lower margin laminate and bedding markets. They suspended dividend payments and were changing their business model to cope with issues in the core business.

While Carpetright had only ~£50 million net debt, it had long-term lease agreements on its stores, ranging from 5 to 15 years. Carpetright had annual rental expense commitments of ~£80 million over the next ten years, which amounted to ~£600 million of debt on a capitalized basis. After accounting for these rental commitments, they had a net debt to earnings before interest, taxes, depreciation, amortization, and rent of 5.5. Carpetright's leverage was not fully apparent on its balance sheet.

Carpetright's same-store sales had been declining since 2006, as shown in figure 3.4; however, this decline was masked by growth from the acquisitions of other retailers. The company's return on invested capital had declined from 56 percent in 2005 to 5 percent in 2011, even though it was still enjoying negative working capital.

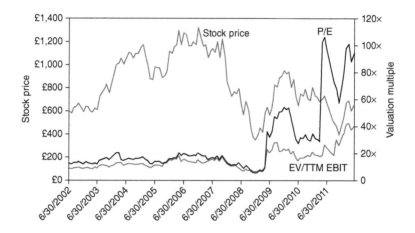

FIGURE 3.2 Carpetright stock price and valuation 2002–2012. *Source:* Carpetright company reports.

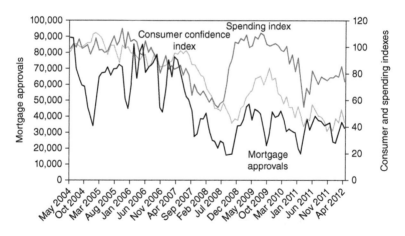

FIGURE 3.3 U.K. macro indicators. *Source:* BBA, TNS-RI, Nationwide.

Carpetright had £26 million in deferred tax liabilities that seemed unlikely to reverse in the absence of sales growth and increases in capital investments. In other words, Carpetright would owe £26 million in taxes if it could not get tax advantage from making capital investments. This could result in a 40 percent loss to shareholder equity.

Carpetright seemed like a value trap, and it was no surprise that the stock had short interest of 18 percent. Interestingly, the stock had a small float due to concentrated positions from a few investors. Lord Harris, the founder and CEO, held 20 percent of the stocks; Franklin Templeton bought a 16 percent stake in 2010 between £600 and £700; Olayan, a Saudi investor group, bought a 15 percent stake in 2003 around £600, and Cascade Limited, Bill Gate's money managers, held 6 percent at an average price between £700 and £800.

The institutional investors were underwater on their investment and wanted a seasoned executive to take over the CEO role from Lord Harris instead of his son, Martin Harris. They recruited Darren Shapland (who was at the time being considered for the CEO position at the largest U.K. supermarket) to replace Lord Harris in May 2012. I published my short thesis on Carpetright in June 2012.

How Did Carpetright Play Out?

The stock lost 10–15 percent of its value a year after I published the report in June 2012. I closed the short position on Carpetright in June 2013.

Other Examples of Value Traps

Value traps and good value stock ideas have a few traits in common. Both may appear cheap on certain valuation metrics, such as P/B and P/E. They tend to have past periods of good financial performance. Other less common traits may include significant cash on the balance sheet, high dividend yields, good historic brand, reputable investors and management, and issues with the core business. Basically, value traps may seem like value stocks, only they are not.

So, what is different? There is no easy answer, but paying attention to downside risks can lead to clues on value traps. These risks can arise from declining profitability in core businesses or diminishing growth prospects. Management can respond to such issues through restructuring or turnaround strategies or by diversifying away from their core business. Stocks of such companies can become potential value traps when management makes an attempt to diversify the business by making overpriced acquisitions, entering a lower margin industry, and launching new products in a highly competitive sector.

Stocks of speculative companies whose turnaround prospects are overly reliant on management reputation, reversal of a down trend in the industry, or success of a key product are also likely to be value traps. Who would not like to buy stocks for cheap? As stock investors, we are wired to look for signs of hope that can reverse the misfortune of cheap stocks.

Value traps can pass the smell test of hope but may not offer definitive signs of defensiveness, brand strength, sustainable earnings, and, most important, limited downside. Such companies can stand to lose their relevance when they are met with a structural change in industry, disruptive technology, and a sea change in regulatory or competitive landscape. Let us take a look at a few notable examples.

Yahoo! reigned as a dominant search engine for five years until 2000 when it was displaced by Google's disruptive new search engine. Yahoo! unsuccessfully attempted to buy Google in 2002 and has never come close to challenging Google since then. Having failed at its core business, Yahoo! made many unsuccessful acquisitions and missed some key acquisitions, namely Facebook and YouTube.

In 2006, Pitney Bowes had 80 percent market share in a highly regulated postal meter market in North America. It had 65 percent market share worldwide and its only major competitor was Neopost. Its business is closely tied to postal mail volumes, which had ranged between 200 and 213 billion pieces per year since 2000. Mail volumes plummeted to 177 billion pieces per year in the 2008 recession, marking the beginning of a secular decline in mail volumes.[4] In 2010, the Boston Consulting Group (BCG) projected mail volumes to decline to 150 billion pieces over the next ten years. BCG believed that the decline was unlikely to reverse because "First-Class Mail is succumbing to the online diversion of bills, invoices, statements, and payments." Pitney Bowes has struggled to offset a decline in revenue by diversifying to more competitive records management and postal software businesses. Its stock declined more than 50 percent since 2011 and its dividend yield increased from 6 percent in 2011 to 13 percent in 2012 as a result of this decline.

Chapter 1 discussed the decline in the personal computer (PC) industry as computers started to become commoditized. The woes of the PC industry have been accentuated by a staggering growth in smartphones and tablets since 2006. The secular decline eventually impacted the top two players, HP and Dell, forcing them to acquire software services businesses and diversify away from PCs. Even proven managers such as Michael Dell and Meg Whitman have not been able to fight the tide of secular decline in the PC industry.

The rise of Internet commerce has led to the demise of many historic icons. Blockbuster suffered from a decline in the DVD rental business and was unable to transition to the new Internet video distribution model. The advertising revenue model for newspapers (McClatchy, Gannett, *New York Times*, etc.) suffered as news distribution shifted to the Internet.

Online retailers have much lower distribution costs and are able to offer much lower prices than traditional retailers. Circuit City,

Linens 'n Things, and many retailers have gone out of business or filed Chapter 11 in recent years. The surviving brick-and-mortar retailers struggle to defend their business model and play catch-up with their own Internet marketplaces in the wake of continued competition from established online retailers. Retailers such as Best Buy and Bed Bath & Beyond have allowed their stores to become virtual showrooms for their online competitors, such as Amazon and eBay.

Takeaway
Disruptive technologies and structural changes in industry growth, competitive landscape, and regulations can virtually destroy the value of a once-successful business, creating potential value traps.

Broken Growth Stories

Unlike value traps, growth stocks may be traded at insanely expensive multiples and will keep getting dearer. Shorting growth stories can be no different than playing with fire, as we saw in the cases of Cisco and Questcor in chapter 1. Shorting growth stocks solely based on high valuation is a sure way to go broke. It is important to identify their drivers of growth, threats to these drivers, and most important, near-term threats. In Questcor's case, we saw that a negative reimbursement policy posed a serious threat to their drug sales; in Cisco's case in 1999, the threats to the company's growth were not obvious.

Companies can find growth from the launch of new products, entry to new markets, and the rise of a new industry or rise in demand. Growing markets, capacity expansion, regulatory changes, and industry consolidation are among many other driv-ers of company growth. It is usually hard to predict a growth hori-zon for a company with long growth runways, and the predictions often become hot debate topics in the media.

However, in some cases, clear signs of threats to a company's growth may arise from disruptive technologies or overcapacity. In other cases, signs of threat may not be as apparent for hot-selling items. Short sellers rely on scuttlebutt, channel checks, surveys, news reports, sell-side research, and industry experts to read the tea leaves.

Regulations such as patent protections, subsidies, and fiscal stimulus usually have limited and clear timeframes. Therefore, it is usually easier to point to threats to a company's growth coming from an expiring regulation or similar impending change.

Broken growth stories can clearly point out issues with growth and growth drivers, profitability, and near-term nega-tive catalysts. The bear thesis must also determine the market size and limitations to the growth of the overall market. Poor financial characteristics (excess leverage, poor coverage ratios, etc.), cracks in the business model, accounting issues, signs of increasing competition, and insider selling are key elements of a good bear case.

CASE STUDY:
SOLAR PANEL MAKERS

The solar industry had come a long way since Bell Laboratories made the first photovoltaic cell in 1954, with costs coming down from $100+ per watt to ~$4 per watt in 2000. Japanese subsidies in the 1990s had helped double global solar installed capacity to 1,000 megawatts. However, solar costs were far from grid parity with electricity produced from conventional sources, such as coal, and the solar industry's competitiveness depended heavily on government subsidies.

The U.S. solar industry could not attract private capital until the enactment of a solar investment tax credit (ITC) in 2006. The cumulative installed capacity in the United States grew from 300 megawatts in 2006 to 800 megawatts in 2008; during the same period, larger subsidies in Germany helped their installed capacity grow from 3,000 megawatts to 6,000 megawatts. Stocks of solar panel makers such as First Solar (FSLR), SunTech Power (STP), and SunPower (SPWR), which supplied these markets, were up 3× to 4× since their initial public offerings (IPOs) by 2008.[5]

However, U.S. tax credits were set to expire in 2008, German subsidies were expected to decline after 2008, and there seemed to be a bump in the solar panel growth story. Margins for the panel makers seemed to be under threat from a flood of new competition. In a January 2008 article I published in *Seeking Alpha*, titled "Bullish on Solar Energy, Bearish on Solar Stocks," I made my short case for the skyrocketing solar stocks. With $300 million in 2007 sales, First Solar was trading at a P/S of 43 ($225) and other panel makers were trading at similarly high multiples. There were signs of cyclical shorting opportunity in the solar sector.

While growth in the solar industry seemed threatened by the uncertain future of subsidies in Germany and the United States, margins were also under threat from a glut in production capacity based on data coming from leading solar associations and research firms. Conversion efficiencies of monocrystalline and multicrystalline silicon for STP ranged between 14 and 16 percent, while that of cadmium telluride for FSLR was even lower at ~10 percent. Competitive panels made from polycrystalline silicon provided 2× to 5× conversion efficiencies and were becoming competitive with the drop in silicon prices.

How Did Solar Stocks Play Out?

The solar panel growth story seemed broken. Uncertain subsidies, increased competition, margin pressure, and alternative polysilicon panels posed a bump to the growth story. High levels of valuation were the icing on the cake for shorting these stocks. Solar stocks fell between 30 and 90 percent in 2008 as the economy worsened. The ITC did not get extended until late 2008, and panel margins declined amid falling average selling prices.

Takeaway

Government subsidies can support fledgling industries in their early stages, and such industries can fail to survive in the absence of subsidies if they fail to create a robust market or generate profitability.

CASE STUDY:
LEAP WIRELESS (LEAP) AND METROPCS (PCS)

Leap Wireless and MetroPCS had raised debt at attractive terms in 2006 to buy spectrum during Federal Communications Commission Auction 36, and each grew their subscriber base by entering new markets. After winning the auction, LEAP entered Chicago and PCS entered Boston and New York; both consequently gained a large number of subscribers from these well-populated markets. LEAP's subscriber base grew from 2.8 million in 2007 to 3.8 million in 2008, and PCS's subscriber base grew from ~4 million in 2007 to 5.3 million in 2008. The market liked their growth story. Their stock prices in March 2009 implied $1,200 to $1,500 of enterprise value per subscriber, compared to the top two players that controlled 80 percent of the wireless market—AT&T and Verizon.

However, LEAP and PCS were prepaid carriers, unlike their postpaid competitors of AT&T, Verizon, and Sprint. Their business model was different because they did not require two-year contracts from their customers like their postpaid competitors did, so they saw a significant churn in their customer bases. Their profit economics were also poor when compared with their peers. Their growth came from entering new markets, which also increased the fixed-cost base from the resulting new cell sites, store costs, salaries, and customer care. Due to these high fixed costs, their profitability is highly dependent on stable average revenue per user (ARPU), subscriber growth, and lower churn (table 3.1).

The return on invested capital to acquire a new wireless customer in the new markets was much lower than in existing markets due to the capital expenditure to build out the new network. LEAP would typically need 6–8 months to break even on acquiring a customer in its existing markets, but twice as long (20+ months) in new markets. To be profitable, LEAP would need to increase its current penetration from 5.7 percent to 9 percent in the wireless markets.

Easy growth for both carriers seemed to near its end as they were expected to complete their rollout by 2010; they would need to challenge the larger carriers to increase their penetration and keep growing. This was difficult for many reasons, primarily because they could not impose long-term contracts on their customers. The other growth option for them would be to acquire additional spectra after they had covered their target population in the new markets in 2010.

Table 3.1
Profit per subscriber and break-even analysis

	New markets		Existing markets	
	PCS	LEAP	PCS	LEAP
Monthly average revenue per unit (ARPU) ($ per month)	38.0	40.0	41.4	42.0
Revenue per year ($)	456.0	480.0	496.7	504.0
Fixed costs per year ($)	(903.9)	(866.4)	(260.0)	(336.0)
Months to break-even	23.8	21.7	6.3	8.0
Annual ROIC (%)	−50	−45	91	50

Source: LEAP and PCS annual and quarterly reports, Artham Capital Partners LLC.

There was more to a bear thesis on their growth and profit-ability. Their grip on the prepaid market was under threat from signs of new competition. Sprint, the third largest carrier, which was still reeling from the poor execution of its recent acquisition of Nextel, had announced that it would enter the prepaid market with cheaper price plans. LEAP and PCS had already cut prices in 2008 to stay competitive in the prepaid market, and new competition meant even lower ARPU. There seemed to be a bump in their growth story.

LEAP and PCS were highly leveraged with a debt to earnings before interest, taxes, depreciation, and amortization (EBITDA) ratio of more than 5.0; their continued losses could quickly lead them to breach their covenant limit of 6–7. While liquidity issues and short-term capital needs did not seem imminent, LEAP and PCS would eventually need to access capital markets and borrow at an even higher rate than their current borrowing rates of 9–10 percent to avoid a disruption in their growth plans.

I had just started my independent research consulting firm in 2009 and published my first short thesis on these two wireless carriers. The biggest risk to my thesis was a merger between LEAP and PCS. After spending four years in bankruptcy prior to 2004, both carriers had been under constant speculation to merge. They had revenue synergies arising from complementary geographies in Las Vegas, Philadelphia, and parts of Chicago, as well as cost synergies from intercarrier agreements. PCS had offered to buy out LEAP in the past, and a merger announcement posed the biggest risk to shorting them.

How Did It Play Out?

On May 28, 2009—much earlier than I had expected—LEAP announced that it would sell 6.1 million shares to raise $240 million and refinance $1.1 billion of loans. LEAP shares declined ~6 percent to $38.74 per share. PCS did not trade down on this news; however, PCS missed its second-quarter estimates in its earnings release on August 6, 2009, and its stock dropped 30 percent to $9 per share. LEAP announced earnings on the same day, reporting higher than expected losses and subscriber churn. LEAP fell 25 percent to $17 per share on the news.

Their shares continued to decline despite repeated merger and acquisition rumors over the next three years, and their poor operating performance outweighed the value of their spectrum. Eventually, T-Mobile announced a reverse merger with PCS in 2012 and AT&T announced that it would acquire LEAP in 2013 for $15 per share in cash.

CASE STUDY:
CHICKEN AND EGG (CHEGG)

One of my clients asked me to look at an upcoming IPO, Chicken and Egg (CHEGG), in late 2013. CHEGG buys textbooks, rents them for two to three years, then depreciates the cost of these books over three years. The company turns around and rents these books at 20–30 percent of the original cost per semester. Essentially, CHEGG could break even in less than 3 years and make 10–15 percent annualized returns on average for its textbook investments.

CHEGG had a subscribed user base of 418,000 students, which is a nearly 10 percent market share of U.S. college students. CHEGG had room to grow its market share by extending its reach. The other source of growth came from bulking up the textbook inventory itself, which would in turn increase their total transaction volume. The company had increased its capital expenditure on buying books by 40 percent to $104 million, and it still had some room to increase the spending to their prior peak spending in 2011 of $134 million. In short, CHEGG seemed to have a poor business model that was capital intensive and generated low returns.

At $213 million in revenue and $23 million in EBITDA, the IPO would occur at an implied valuation of 5x sales and 25x EBITDA based on midpoint of indicative pricing. It seemed expensive at first glance, despite its growth opportunities in e-books and others. I recommended against my client participating in the IPO; however, I recognized a key risk to my thesis.

The only risk I saw with betting against CHEGG was that its business model lends well as a target acquisition to the likes of Amazon, who can extract more value out of the business model by utilizing their efficient logistics operations and technology platform. That said, it was hard to imagine a bid from Amazon on the day of CHEGG's IPO.

CHEGG's IPO was not very successful, falling 25 percent on IPO and continuing to fall another 30 percent over next six months.

Takeaway

Broken growth stories can clearly point out issues with growth and growth drivers, profitability, and near-term negative catalysts and events. Takeover is the leading risk with shorting stocks.

Recap

- Companies may suffer significant blows to their business model, which may be irreparable. For example, their growth story may be broken as a result of disruptive products, competition, or the value of their business being on a structural decline.
- The collapse in the subprime mortgage market permanently changed the business model of the financial services industry, and demand for related securitized products collapsed. Tightening credit cycles and tougher regulations ensued, suppressing profitability in the financial sector.
- Disruptive technologies and structural changes in industry growth, competitive landscape, and regulations can severely destroy the value of a once-successful business.
- Broken growth stories can clearly point out issues with growth and growth drivers, profitability, and near-term negative catalysts and events. Takeover is the leading risk with shorting stocks.

4

Recipes for Cooked Books

Accounting Misstatements and Shenanigans

The least initial deviation from the truth is multiplied later
a thousandfold.
—ARISTOTLE

FINANCIAL ACCOUNTING IS THE LANGUAGE of both private and
public companies. Companies often use poetic license to infringe
on elements of accounting rules. Their intention or lack of intention behind minor misstatements or outright misrepresentations
can be hard to determine ex-post for the jury and even harder
to determine ex-ante for investors. However, it is possible for
investors to analyze the often-misused accounting methods and
assumptions to detect early warning signs.

This chapter assumes that readers are familiar with basic
accounting concepts and generally accepted accounting principles
(GAAP). GAAP relies on the premise that accrual accounting provides more useful information than cash accounting. Unlike cash
accounting, accrual accounting is based on the concept of revenue
recognition and matching revenues with expenses in an accounting period. Accrual accounting allows management to make reasonable assumptions on how and when to record these revenues
and expenses.

Accounting principles allow management to make assumptions on many other transactions, such as classifying investment assets, testing goodwill impairment, choosing depreciation methods, estimating the life of depreciable assets, reporting liabilities off the balance sheet, and so on. We saw earlier how AIG chose to price its investments based on its own assumptions as opposed to the prevailing market prices of comparable assets.

More importantly, accounting guidelines allow management considerable latitude in making changes to their assumptions and frequent changes at times. Consequently, management can make ad-hoc decisions regarding changes in their accounting assumptions which may not necessarily be triggered by changes in accounting standards or changes in the way their company conducts business. In certain cases, management can switch to more favorable assumptions to improvise their financial and operating metrics and paint a better picture of their company's financial health and future prospects. We will look at some of the common recipes for cooked books in this chapter.

Key Reasons Behind Financial Restatements

The most common reasons behind restatements include revenue recognition, expense overstatement or understatement, misclassifications, mergers and acquisitions, restructuring, and derivatives accounting. Companies can misclassify items in any or all of the three key financial statements. For example, a company may state an operating cash outflow item as financial cash outflow on the cash flow statement, misclassify a capital asset lease as an operating lease, or misclassify gain from a sale as revenue.

In its 2002 report, "Financial Statement Restatements," the U.S. General Accounting Office (GAO) reported that more than 50 percent of accounting restatements made between 1997 and

2002 resulted from improper revenue and cost accounting. Four years after the 2002 enactment of the Sarbanes-Oxley Act, the GAO reported that 55 percent of the restatements between 2002 and 2005 resulted from revenue and cost improprieties.[1]

Companies are forced to restate their financial statements after these accounting improprieties are discovered by internal or external parties. The restating company stands to suffer permanent damage to its stock price and reputation, and it may even cause its competitors to face loss of confidence and increased scrutiny from investors.

Changes in Assumptions Can Be the Most Critical Warning Signs

Investors can detect accounting issues by paying attention to unusual assumptions and changes in assumptions used in reporting financial statements. For example, a bank can decide to change its time period assumptions to redefine nonperforming assets, or a company can choose to report a large normal loss as a one-time extraordinary loss based on the assumption that the loss is unlikely to occur again. Accounting issues can only be uncovered by the old-fashioned way of scrutinizing financial statements, so let us take a look at some common accounting assumptions that affect the operating metrics and profitability of a company. Changes and anomalies in the assumptions can often point to early warning signs.

How Is the Revenue Booked?

Sell-in versus sell-through: When companies sell their products through indirect channels such as distributors and retailers, sell-in can allow companies to book revenues early. For example, Incyte decided in 2012 to recognize revenues when the pharmacy received its product (sell-in) versus when the pharmacy sent its product to the patient (sell-through).[2]

Revenues versus deferred revenue: When companies record customer advances as deferred revenues and recognize them as revenue over the estimated product life, shorter life assumptions allow companies to book revenues early. For example,[3] Apple assumed a 24-month product life for its devices until 2009 when it elected to adopt changes to revenue recognition standards for multiple deliverables. Consequently, Apple could book a substantial portion of device revenues at the time of sale.

Sale-type lease versus operating lease: When companies offer customers the option to lease their products, they commonly record the leases as operating leases or sales-type leases. A sales-type lease allows companies to record a higher gain and lower assets at the time of sale because they can lower their cost of goods by the estimated residual value. For example, Tesla announced a lease financing program for electric cars in 2013, with a guaranteed resale value higher than that of any other luxury sedan.[4] High resale value could allow Tesla to book higher profits.

How Are Expenses Classified?

Cost of goods (LIFO versus FIFO inventory accounting): When companies sell inventory, they can choose the last-in/first-out (LIFO) or first-in/first-out (FIFO) method to record the cost of goods sold. Companies disclose any related LIFO reserves and do not change their choice of inventory accounting without prior notification to investors. FIFO accounting allows companies to record a lower cost of goods during periods of rising inventory costs as compared to LIFO.

Capital lease versus operating lease: When companies record long-term leases on real estate, vehicles, and other major assets as operating leases, they do not record a related financial obligation on the balance sheet, unlike capital leases. Operating leases allow companies to post better returns on capital. The Financial Accounting Standards Board is considering an overhaul to lease accounting that would mandate lessees to recognize assets and liabilities for leases of more than one year.[5] We saw an example of this in chapter 3 when Office Depot chose operating lease accounting for its long-term leases.

Sales and marketing costs versus deferred acquisition costs (similar to operating expense versus capital expenditures): When companies aggressively spend on sales and marketing or pay large upfront commissions to selling agents or brokers, they can choose to capitalize such expenses as deferred costs and amortize them over a longer period. This allows them to lower and smooth their expenses. For example, insurance companies amortize deferred costs based on their estimate of gross profits on an insurance contract.

Do Balance Sheet Items Adequately Provision for Losses and Write-Downs?

Inventory (raw material price): When the pricing of its product is tied to commodity prices, a company needs to perform an impairment test in the wake of falling commodity prices and may be required to increase reserves or write-down inventories. For example, gold miners and fertilizer producers have had to write down inventories amid falling prices.

Inventory (market price): Management has a lot of discretion over the timing of impairment tests and the estimation of inventory reserves. This can also allow management to write up new or used inventory. Companies tend to build up excess inventory when they anticipate the success of a new product launch; however, the value of inventory would need to be written down if sales fail to meet expectations and the company begins offering steep discounts. For example, Skechers built excess inventory of their hot-selling Shape-Ups in 2010 and did not recognize the problem of excess inventory for more than a couple of quarters.[6]

Accounts receivable: When a company derives significant sales from a few customers, provides financing to buy its products, or collects cash a few months after delivering a product or service, it would need to increase the allowance for bad debts when their customers face deteriorating business or credit conditions. While the company itself may have a good credit standing, it is vulnerable to tightening credit conditions for its customers as well. For example, the Circuit City bankruptcy in 2008 led Garmin to increase their allowance for bad debt expense.[7]

Goodwill and intangible assets: When companies complete mergers or acquisitions, they record the amount they paid in excess of fair value for their target as goodwill and other intangibles. Higher goodwill and intangibles allow companies to understate book value of equity and report higher returns on equity, and also allow management to overpay for acquisitions when organic growth is hard to come by. Goodwill and intangibles are subject to impairment tests just like inventories, and management usually writes them down when mergers prove disastrous. For example, HP blamed accounting improprieties at Autonomy prior to its acquisition of Autonomy to write down related $8.8 billion of goodwill and intangibles in 2012.[8]

Deferred tax assets and liabilities: Companies can make different assumptions for certain accounting items when they report to tax authorities versus investors; the resulting temporary differences may not reverse in the near future. Growth companies may assume accelerated depreciation for fixed assets and keep deferring more tax expenses. However, deferred tax liabilities begin to reverse once growth disappears and have a negative impact on the book value of equity. We saw an example of this in chapter 3, when Carpetright's deferred tax liabilities of £28 million were at risk of becoming a liability in the absence of sales growth and increase in capital expenditures.

Do Balance Sheet Items Represent Fair Market Values?

Investment assets (historical cost versus marked-to-market): Companies can choose to record their investment assets at historical costs (held-to-maturity) or mark them to market (classified as available for sale and trading). A held-to-maturity classification allows companies to avoid reporting changes in the market value of their assets. For example, when commercial banks underwrite loans, they can record them as held-to-maturity assets (also called loan-book). They can reclassify these loans as available for sale or trading assets (also called trading-book) to lower their regulatory capital requirement.

Fair-value hierarchy of assets and liabilities (levels 1, 2, and 3 inputs): When companies report the fair value of assets and liabilities, they can use market quotes for identical assets (level 1 input), similar assets (level 2 input), or use their own assumptions, which are not observable in the market (level 3 inputs). We saw an example of this in chapter 3 when AIG (and other financial institutions) chose to report the value of certain liabilities and assets based on financial models that used their own input assumptions.

Off-balance sheet items and contingent liabilities: Companies may not report certain contractual commitments, derivative-related liabilities, and other contingent liabilities on the balance sheet but disclose them separately. For example, Disney had contractual commitments of $42.8 billion to buy broadcast rights for sports in 2012. Banks may have an untapped line of credit as contingent liabilities.[9] Manufacturing and mining companies may not have accrued liabilities for pending environmental damage complaints.

Litigation and damages: Regulators can file charges on companies for a variety of reasons, such as antitrust issues, consumer fraud, and foreign bribery. In other cases, courts may issue adverse verdicts and find companies liable for related damages. In both cases, companies may choose not to make provisions for damages in their financial statement and appeal their cases, wherein the appeals process may take months or years to complete. For example, the jury found Marvell Technology liable for $1.17 billion in a patent infringement lawsuit brought by Carnegie Mellon University; however, Marvell decided to challenge the verdict and not accrue related liabilities.[10] In a different case, the U.S. Department of Justice sued Standard & Poor (S&P) for $5 billion in damages for fraud in rating Mortgage Backed Securities (MBS) while S&P decided to defend itself and not accrue any reserves for the litigation.

Are Other Financial Statements Diverging from Income Statements?

Net income versus cash flow from operations: As companies mature in their growth cycle, net income and cash flow from operations begin to converge as depreciation expenses and working capital needs stabilize. Wide variations between net income and cash flow from operations merit a closer look at the noncash items that are behind the divergence.

Net income versus other comprehensive income: Net income and other comprehensive income are like left and right pockets of the company financials. Companies can choose to present components of net income and comprehensive income in a continuous statement or as separate items. Companies usually report unrealized gains and losses on hedges, available-for-sale investment assets, adjustments for pension plans, and foreign exchange translation gains and losses in comprehensive income. In particular, banks are in the business of trading securities, and any related gains and losses merit a closer look.

Takeaway
Revenue and expense assumptions impact profitability. Companies may not adequately provision for losses in both cash and noncash balance sheet items. Off-balance sheet commitments can hide leverage.

Next Step: Do the Operating Metrics Pass the Smell Test?

Operating metrics related to profit margins, returns, liquidity, turnover, and leverage are good measures to check a company's pulse. These ratios can understate or overstate the operating performance of a company and may often need to be adjusted to show a clearer picture of the company's performance.

Profit Margins

Gross margins versus operating margins: Companies can choose to classify certain expenses related to depreciation or employee wages as part of the inventory costs. When companies decide to reclassify such expenses, the resulting margins may not be comparable to prior-year margins. Margins would need to be adjusted for reclassification in such a case. In other cases, companies may shift to licensing or franchising models, which shift the cost of inventory to the licensee and allows the company to boost operating margins. Companies disclose their system-wide sales, including franchise sales and license fees, which can be used to adjust the overall sales and margins, and examine if franchising is accretive to margins.

Returns

Return on capital or net income/invested capital: This is an important metric to measure the economic value generated by a company. Companies may destroy economic value when their returns fall short of their cost of capital. As we saw in the case of operating leases, companies can move assets off-balance sheet or outsource production to overstate their return on capital. When it is not possible to adjust for off-balance sheet items, we can look at comparable companies to see if the returns are abnormally high or low.

Return on equity or net income/equity: This can be analyzed using the DuPont model (Return on equity = Net income margin × Asset turnover × Leverage) to determine the contribution of profit margins, operating leverage, and financial leverage to overall returns. Companies often tend to overpay for growth and margin accretion during acquisitions and record overpayments as goodwill on the balance sheet. Goodwill allows the company to overstate equity and understate leverage. We can use tangible equity or book value adjusted for goodwill to examine if acquisitions mask poor past returns.

Liquidity or Ability to Service Short-Term Debt

Cash ratio (or cash/current liabilities): This is the most conservative measure of liquidity and excludes accounts receivable and inventories, which may not be readily converted into cash. When companies become unprofitable or incur heavy debt, their liquidity needs are closely tied to payables and debt maturity schedules. Companies can resolve liquidity issues by securitizing their accounts receivable, negotiating payment terms with suppliers, and tapping lines of credit or capital markets. Cash ratio and cash conversion cycle trends are prognostic indicators of impending liquidity issues.

Turnover

Receivables turnover and inventory turnover: These trends can help detect unusual build-up in inventory and channel-stuffing issues. Consumer and industrial companies can ship extra inventory to distribution channels and inflate revenues—a practice known as channel stuffing. As previously discussed, companies often end up marking down receivables and inventories when they are not able to move channel inventory or make cash collections.

Leverage

Interest coverage ratio, debt/EBITDA, and debt/equity: Companies are usually required to comply with debt covenant requirements for these three key ratios. Credit agreements can be complicated if they involve multiple loan tranches or when debt is secured by collateral such as company assets. When a company's debt service ratio is precariously close to covenant requirements, the company can possibly enter the zone of insolvency by defaulting on loans, accruing interest payments, or filing for bankruptcy. Poor ratios can raise alarms about credit issues and merit a detailed credit analysis of the company.

Takeaway
Operating metrics related to profit margins, returns, liquidity, turnover, and leverage are good measures to check a company's pulse. Trends in these metrics can provide early indications of an impending issue.

Look for Trends in Industry-Specific Metrics

Companies disclose industry-specific metrics to provide a better picture of operating performance to their investors. These metrics can allow investors to make better comparisons with other companies in the industry. Industry metrics are usually based on actual numbers; however, they can be based on management estimates as well. Examples include bank nonperforming assets (NPAs), such as nonaccrual loans, impaired loans, and restructured loans. Management may not place certain consumer or credit card loans in nonaccrual status prior to charging them off. We can examine if banks are reporting lower NPAs in comparison to NPAs during past recessions. NPAs provide early clues of a downturn when the credit cycle begins to tighten.

We saw earlier that similar assumptions on revenue recognition can impact even the most basic revenue drivers, such as unit price and volume shipped. If we assume that timing issues related to management assumptions will smooth out over longer periods, we can examine cyclical trends in these industry-specific metrics. Table 4.1 summarizes the commonly watched industry metrics that can provide more information on business cycle trends.

Which Operating Metrics Drive Executive Compensation?

Executive compensation can be tied to GAAP metrics such as earnings per share (EPS) and operating margins, as well as non-GAAP metrics, such as the industry-specific metrics. Why is it important to pay attention to these metrics? As we saw in the case of Office Depot, the board set a low bar by tying management incentives to positive EBITDA. In addition, the board guaranteed bonuses to key executives upon approval of preferred share conversions in BC Partners' private investment in public equity transaction that triggered change of control provisions in executive employment contracts.

Executives will likely pursue strategies and decisions that are favorable to the operating metrics driving their performance targets and bonuses. For example, when the board ties incentives to return on invested capital, management may choose to enter sale leaseback transactions to divest assets and lighten the capital base. In other cases, executives may choose to outsource production if their incentives are tied to gross margins.

Performance targets for these metrics can provide insight into the strategies that the management is likely to pursue. However, boards can also set vague performance targets that are tied to

Table 4.1
Key industry-specific metrics

Industry sector	Key metrics
Airlines	Available seat miles, load factor
Banks	NPAs, capital ratios, net interest margins (NIMs), asset quality metrics
Energy and mining	Cash production costs, reserves, and reserve replacement ratio
Hotels and restaurants	Revenues per available room (RevPAR), occupancy rates, average daily rate; restaurants disclose average ticket size, volumes other than retail metrics
Industrials	Order book, backlog, book-to-bill ratios, capacity utilization
Insurance companies	Claims and expense ratio, statutory surplus, investment asset quality metrics
Media and telecom	Net additions, ARPU, churn (subscription businesses disclose similar metrics)
Refiners	Crack spread, WTI-Brent crude oil spread, plant utilization
REITS	Occupancy, rent per square foot, cap rate, releasing spread, free funds flow
Retailers	Same-store sales or like for like (LFL); also comparable store sales or comps, store openings and closures

Source: Artham Capital Partners LLC.

qualitative factors and one or more of thirty metrics. In such cases, it is harder to gauge management's motivation to pursue one important strategy versus another.

Are There Any Unusual Financial Transactions?

Companies can sometimes enter special transactions such as securitizing their accounts receivable, setting up special leasing companies to sell their products, and making transformational acquisitions. Such transactions may alter the company's business model, and it is important to pay attention to the impacted operating metrics.

It is even more important to pay attention to special financial transactions, such as when a company issues debt to make special dividend payments to its shareholders or when a company does a reverse stock split to attract institutional investors. Such transactions may simply turn out to be financial gimmicks and do nothing to improve operating performance in the least.

Uncovering Accounting Problems Is Only Half the Battle

As we have seen in this chapter, companies may make unreasonable assumptions or engage in financial shenanigans to overstate operating performance or understate financial risks. In more extreme cases, management can cover up business problems by misstating financial statements or making frequent business acquisitions. However, uncovering such accounting issues is only half the battle.

The other half lies in finding issues with the business model; not all accounting issues end up in frauds and bankruptcies. In August 2013, I was asked by a client for my opinion on Precision Castparts (PCP), which had been recommended as a potential short by an accounting forensic company—primarily because of

PCP's accounting treatment of inventory reserves. PCP recorded 95 percent of its inventories on a LIFO basis, and some analysts believed that the carrying value may be high. The LIFO costing method matches the current costs with current sales, and it could allow PCP to boost EPS by using low prevailing metal prices.

Average prices for key metal inputs (nickel, titanium, and cobalt) had declined 20–40 percent in the last couple of years and the raw materials portion of PCP's inventory has grown from $437 million to $903 million during that period. PCP's recent acquisition of TIMET had added a total $778 million of inventory at fair value, of which approximately $200 million was raw materials. Therefore, approximately $270 million of PCP's inventory ($903 million – $437 million – $200 million) could be subject to 20–40 percent write-down, which translated to a maximum of $80 million of one-time inventory write-downs. PCP had a market capitalization of approximately $30 billion, so this write-down seemed too low to cause a significant dent to the EPS or stock price.

While PCP's cyclically high margins, near-term issues related to Boeing 747, and a possible macroeconomic downturn could make a case for tactical shorting, PCP did not seem to be structural short or a long-term short for several reasons. Commercial aviation market recovery and continued increase in Boeing 787 production rates were tailwinds to PCP's organic growth. PCP sells more than $10 million of content for every 787, Boeing's new and fast-growing airplane model, making it hard to question management's outlook for organic growth. I recommended against short selling PCP.

CASE STUDY:
DIAMOND FOODS (DMND)

When Off Wall Street noticed issues with Diamond's accounting treatment of its prospective "momentum payment" paid to walnut growers in 2011, it suspected that Diamond was overstating profitability by trying to book the payment as a one-time integration cost. Diamond, a walnut cooperative, paid its growers 10–15 percent less than fair market price for walnuts. As purchase agreements with walnut suppliers signed at the time of the IPO expired, DMND risked losing suppliers and decided to make up for it with a one-time payment. The business problem at the root of this accounting problem prompted Off Wall Street to look for other issues with the business model.

Diamond appeared to be losing its dominant position in the walnut industry. As a result, its business model was deteriorating and its profitability was under pressure. Management understood the problem and was trying to diversify and grow its business through acquisitions. However, their latest announcement to acquire Pringles bore integration risks. Pringles also had weak growth prospects as a small player with a mature product in a very competitive snack market dominated by Frito-Lay. Earnings estimates appeared too high as well.

How Did It Play Out?

Diamond stock fell more than 80 percent to $14 as the Pringles deal fell through and the company struggled to repair its reputation after restating its financials.

Source: Off Wall Street.

Recap

• **Start with key accounting assumptions to detect warning signs**

  o **Revenues**

    ▪ **Sell-in versus sell-through**
    ▪ **Revenues versus deferred revenue**
    ▪ **Sale-type lease versus operating lease**

o Expenses

- Cost of goods (LIFO vs. FIFO inventory accounting)
- Capital lease versus operating lease
- Sales and marketing costs versus deferred acquisition costs

o Balance sheet items

- Inventory (effect of market price and raw material cost)
- Accounts receivable
- Goodwill and intangibles
- Deferred tax assets and liabilities
- Investment assets classification
- Investment assets fair market value assumptions
- Off-balance sheet liabilities

o Divergence between income statement and other statements
o Key metrics, executive compensation, and unusual activities

- Gross and operating margins
- Returns on capital and equity
- Cash ratio, cash conversion cycle, and free cash flow
- Receivable and inventory turnover ratios
- Debt covenant metrics and other leverage ratios

5

The World Is Going to End

It's a recession when your neighbor loses his job; it's a depression
when you lose your own.
—HARRY S. TRUMAN

ON BLACK WEDNESDAY (September 16, 1992), George Soros's
Quantum fund made over $1 billion on his short bet on the British
pound. Soros bet that the pound would pull out of the European
Exchange Rate Mechanism (ERM). Germany was raising interest
rates to combat inflationary pressures after reunification with East
Germany, while the United Kingdom reeled from a recession.[1]

The United Kingdom was a weak link in the ERM. Soros saw
that rates would continue to diverge and force the Bank of England
to abandon the ERM and devalue the pound. Nearly twenty years
later, the Euro, the unified European currency, faced a similar fate
as Portugal, Ireland, Greece, and Spain proved to be the weak links.
These countries went out of step with target debt and deficit levels for
Eurozone nations, heightening fears that the Euro could break up.

During these economic crises, successful investors often said,
"All correlations go to one during crisis." Simply put, there is
no place to hide during a crisis. You cannot avoid losses by
switching from stocks to bonds, bonds to currencies, speculative
stocks to defensive stocks, or junk bonds to investment-grade

98

bonds. Even your cash in the bank may be unsafe during a systemic banking crisis.

While you struggle to cut losses with the sky falling and bears growling on television, you cannot help but notice the schadenfreude among smart investors and some lucky ones who actually made windfall profits from the crisis. You realize that these investors had either shorted the market (stocks, bonds, currencies, derivatives, etc.) or bought some form or another of crisis insurance, such as put options, credit default swaps (CDSs), and other complex derivatives.

While you can make profits many more times than the premium paid for these insurance-like products, you may not be eligible to buy CDSs and other similar instruments that are available only to institutional investors. However, you have the option to short stocks and buy puts to profit from the crisis or simply sell out to cut your losses.

The larger goal is to predict signs of an upcoming crisis and understand the severity of an ongoing crisis. There is no easy answer, but history stores many events, which tend to rhyme.

History Rhymes

Let us look at some major corrections in the S&P 500 since 1929 and the reasons behind them (table 5.1). The underlying reasons behind past crises tend to reappear in different forms and provide clues to the depth of an impending crisis and corrections in the stock market.

CASE STUDY:
LEHMAN FILES BANKRUPTCY IN 2008, UNITED
STATES LOSES AAA IN 2011, S&P 500 MOVES

On Friday, August 5, 2011, I was not sure if the U.S. credit would be downgraded, but I was sure that a potential downgrade would likely be a tail event. I went back to take another look at the market

Table 5.1
Major corrections in the S&P 500 since 1929

Year	Peak-to-trough correction	Event description
1929 crash	–45%	Great Depression, Part I
1930–1931 crash	–86%	Great Depression, Part II
1937 crash	–54%	Great Depression, Part III
1946	–27%	Post–World War II contraction
1957	–20%	Business recession
1962	–27%	May 29th flash crash
1966	–21%	Credit crunch
1973–1974 crash	–48%	Oil shock, Bretton Woods collapse
1987 crash	–33%	Mother of flash crashes
1990	–18%	Iraqi invasion of Kuwait, Gulf
1998	–20%	Russian default, Long-Term Capital Management
2000–2002	–49%	Technology crash
2008–2009	–57%	Great Recession, financial crisis
2010	–16%	Euro crisis begins
2011	–20%	U.S. credit downgrade

Source: S&P Dow Jones indices, Bloomberg.

reaction during the week of the last major tail event, the Lehman bankruptcy in 2008. The S&P 500 closed at 1251.7 on the Friday (September 12, 2008) leading up to Lehman's bankruptcy and dropped 60 points on the Monday following their bankruptcy. While this marked the beginning of the biggest market decline in the last 75 years, the market had recouped all the losses from the Lehman event just one week later on September 19, closing at 1255.08—helped by two strong rallies.

It was déjà vu all over again in 2011, when the S&P 500 fell 80 points on the Monday after S&P stripped the United States of its AAA rating. Over the week, the S&P 500 followed the same price chart as each consecutive day after the Lehman bankruptcy in 2008, falling and rising by almost the same number of points. The S&P 500 rhymed.

The S&P 500's wild moves in 2008 and 2011 were triggered by similar events. On September 15, 2008, markets were hit by more bad news: S&P downgraded AIG's credit rating, following through on its prior threat to downgrade AIG. Likewise, S&P made no exception in 2011 when it followed through on its threat to downgrade the U.S. credit rating from AAA to AA+. History rhymed, but was this as deep a crisis or a black swan event like the Lehman bankruptcy?

Takeaway
If the AIG downgrade was a prologue, it seemed probable that S&P would downgrade the United States' rating as well. Ex-post, it was reasonable to speculate wild swings in the S&P 500. History often repeats itself—when it does, past performance in the stock market can offer clues to what may result from current events.

Was the U.S. Credit Downgrade a Black Swan Event?

In theory, the U.S. credit downgrade should have caused the cost of capital to go up because the risk-free rate was now based on the yield of a AA+ security. Consequently, the price multiples would have been expected to shrink. In reality, the impact of the U.S. credit downgrade on credit and stock markets was a tale of two cities: the S&P 500 declined by 80 points on the news as one would expect; however, U.S. Treasury and bond prices soared.

The U.S. downgrade was not a normal economic event; however, it was not quite a black swan event either. What were the odds of a credit crunch, liquidity crunch, or a 50 percent correction in the stock markets given that the U.S. Federal Reserve ("the Fed") was on standby to continue quantitative easing (QE) and keep interest rates low for an extended period of time? Low odds indeed.

The S&P downgrade had not yet led to a funding and liquidity squeeze or any liquidation or fire sales remotely close to what transpired after Lehman, and the Fed seemed well prepared to provide liquidity this time around. Stock markets had corrected ~13 percent in a knee-jerk reaction during the week of the downgrade; however, credit markets showed few signs of distress, with treasury yields hitting an all-time low. Continued gloominess from Europe, poor economic indicators in the United States, and fears of a China slowdown could tip the U.S. economy into recession, but no black swan event was in sight.

A U.S. default on its obligations or the breakup of the Euro had a greater chance of being a black swan event; however, both the cans were kicked down the road after the compromise on the U.S. debt ceiling and the bailout of Greece. The Fed delivered on expectations, announcing that it would keep rates at zero until 2013.

U.S. Downgrade in 2011 Versus Japan Downgrade in 2001

S&P had downgraded the United States for the first time in its history, and the longer-term impact of the downgrade remained a question. If we looked in the rearview mirror at Japan's downgrade in 2001 for cues, we would find some similarities. For starters, the Japanese yields declined as an initial reaction to the credit downgrade in 2001, just like U.S. treasury yields.

In this context, Japan's central bank policy actions also offered clues for the markets. Japan's rates were already near zero in 2001, just like the U.S. rates in 2011. The Bank of Japan (BOJ), Japan's central bank, chose the path of QE or balance sheet expansion, increasing the circulation of yen banknotes after the downgrade. The BOJ could not have lowered rates below zero.

Over the next five years, BOJ assets as a percent of Japanese gross domestic product (GDP) nearly doubled, from 15 percent to ~30 percent. During these five years, the yen lost value and the Japanese economy showed abysmal signs of growth. Japanese stocks jumped in response to BOJ policy actions, and BOJ began to tighten its balance sheet at the end of 2005. However, the financial crisis in the United States forced BOJ to reverse course and restart balance sheet expansion.

We could follow these cues in history to infer that the U.S. economy was headed nowhere, while the bulls argued that the U.S. economy was inherently stronger than the Japanese economy and did not suffer from structural issues, such as the aging population in Japan. Despite the dissimilarities between the United States and Japan, it seemed evident that U.S. equity and credit markets would continue to be focused on the central bank's policy actions.

While you are left to wonder if the U.S. economy would follow a course similar to Japan's over the next ten years, you could turn to a more predictable variable: Ben Bernanke, the chairman of the U.S. Federal Reserve.

Ben Bernanke on Japan's Lost Decade and the U.S. Great Depression

Bernanke had indicated in the past that an early end to expansionary monetary policies and/or a lack of expansionary policy were key reasons behind the Great Depression of the 1930s and Japan's lost decade of growth in the 1990s. He had studied both events at length and published reports that had been analyzed to death by economists, investors, and analysts.[2]

In his 1994 paper, "The Macroeconomics of the Great Depression: A Comparative Approach," Bernanke compared the behavior of selected macro variables in countries that left the gold standard during the depression to those that did not. He concluded the following: "(1) monetary contraction was an important source of the Depression in all countries; (2) subsequent to 1931 or 1932, there was a sharp divergence between countries which remained on the gold standard and those that left it; and (3) this divergence arose because countries leaving the gold standard had greater freedom to initiate expansionary monetary policies."[3]

Later, in 2003, Bernanke remarked on BOJ:

> I would like to consider an important institutional issue, which is the relationship between the condition of the Bank of Japan's balance sheet and its ability to undertake more aggressive monetary policies. Although, in principle, balance-sheet considerations should not seriously constrain central bank policies, in practice they do. However, as I will discuss, relatively simple measures that would eliminate this constraint are available.[4]

As his simple measure suggested, "The BOJ might have to scrap rules that it has set for itself; for example, its informal rule that the quantity of long-term government bonds on its balance sheet must be kept below the outstanding balance of banknotes issued."

If Bernanke did not find BOJ's decision to increase the balance sheet assets by 30 percent to be aggressive enough, it was safe to infer that he would not hit the brakes and continue with the grand expansionary policy in the United States that began in 2007.

Did the Lenders of Last Resort
Have Room to Lend?

Central bankers (also known as lenders of last resort) at the Fed, BOJ, and the European Central Bank (ECB) printed currencies to expand balance sheets, funding nearly 20 percent of respective GDPs and remaining committed to lending more. It seemed in line with Bernanke's earlier suggestion to eliminate constraints on expanding the balance sheet.

Chronologically, Japan was first among equals: Japan had increased its balance sheet from 20 percent to 30 percent of its GDP over five years since the 2001 downgrade, while keeping their benchmark rates below 1 percent. It was déjà vu a decade later as the Fed renewed its commitment to lend at zero percent over the next two years and fueled the speculation of further expansion of the balance sheet or QE.

The U.S. Federal Reserve was in a similar position as Japan with zero interest rates, two rounds of quantitative easing, and assets at 20 percent of GDP. The Federal Reserve had not held such a high level of assets since World War II. If Bernanke used his own prescription to eliminate constraints on expanding the balance sheet, another round of QE would have been no surprise.

The impact of the Eurozone crisis on U.S. markets had turned the spotlight on ECB. ECB always had a larger balance sheet than the Federal Reserve since the formation of the Euro in 1999. They had expanded the balance sheet just like the Fed (figure 5.1), to above 20 percent of the GDP after the Lehman crisis.

Despite criticisms of ECB's large balance sheet, ECB had room to further expand its balance sheet in response to more market fear. ECB's monopoly on issuance of Euros and other policy tools could allow them to act swiftly if Germany and France were willing. After the 2011 Greece crisis, ECB saw its balance sheet soar to almost 25 percent of the Eurozone GDP. ECB was essentially following the lead from BOJ and the U.S. Fed.

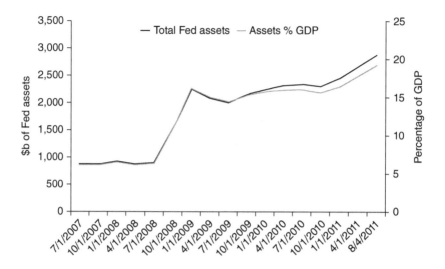

FIGURE 5.1 Fed balance sheet expansion after two rounds of QE. *Source:* Federal Reserve.

If BOJ monetary policy was a guidepost, ECB and the Fed balance sheet still had room to grow in terms of balance sheet assets as a percent of their GDP. Central banks had expanded their balance sheets to all-time highs; however, their monopoly to print unlimited currency made them seem unstoppable. Central banks had diminished the possibility of a liquidity crunch.

Central Banks Flushed Out Liquidity Risk but Left Credit Risk Lingering

Without any hawkish signals from the central banks, the case to short sell based on liquidity issues was weak. However, a U.S. credit downgrade could still lead to credit issues and raise funding costs for companies that were heavily dependent on credit markets. Banks are especially vulnerable to issues in the credit market and rising funding costs because they depend on the wholesale funding markets. Banks with poor loan quality and regulatory capital issues are even more exposed to a drop in profitability. Let us look at Regions Financial, a short idea that I published in July 2011.

CASE STUDY:
REGIONS FINANCIAL (RF)

On June 23, 2011, Regions Financial reached a $200 million settlement with the Securities and Exchange Commission for charges that Morgan Keegan, a brokerage unit of Regions, defrauded customers during the financial crisis.[5] Regions is a diversified commercial bank operating in the southeastern United States, with a majority of operations in Florida, Tennessee, Alabama, Georgia, and Mississippi (figure 5.2). Regions also announced to sell Morgan Keegan to raise money to repay its government Troubled Asset Relief Program(TARP)-preferred stocks from the 2008 financial crisis. I had followed Regions in the past and decided to look at any funding issues.

While Regions was not exposed to a rise in funding costs with $4 billion in short term borrowings and a loan-to-deposit ratio below 100 percent, it needed to boost its Tier 1 regulatory capital. Because Regions had more than $50 billion in assets, it could also face potential systemic risk capital burden, which could be introduced under the new Basel III banking regulations.[6]

Regions was adversely exposed to home equity loans secured by second liens in Florida, which accounted for ~8 percent of their total loan portfolio. Their nonperforming assets (NPAs) or loans past due by 90 days or more had stayed stubbornly high at 4 percent and its Texas ratio (percent of NPAs covered by equity and loss reserve provisions) was at 57 percent. Poor-quality loans could erase half of the book value of the company's equity. I had stumbled onto a potential short idea.

Regions had $1.4 billion in net deferred tax assets, of which $424 million was disallowed for Tier 1. Region's decision to sell Morgan Keegan would have eased the pressure to raise capital,

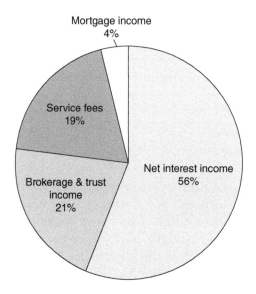

FIGURE 5.2 2010 revenues $6.5 billion. *Source:* RF reports.

but Regions also wanted to repay their $3.5 billion of government TARP preferred stocks. Morgan Keegan's estimated sale at $1.5 billion would not have fetched even half the capital to repay TARP and tough market conditions could lower the sale price. Regions shareholders faced a dilution risk.

Morgan Keegan's sale would have also resulted in a loss of revenues in excess of $1 billion per year and $70–100 million lower net income, and Regions' reliance on interest income would increase significantly after the sale. In addition, Dodd-Frank regulation changes could result in a loss of $150–170 million in debit card income.

Regions faced an overhang from its TARP-preferred stocks, poor asset quality, reduced normalized earnings power, and other short-term negative catalysts, such as headline risk of their ongoing board investigation into their credit practices that could result in additional settlement expenses. Regions should have traded below a price/tangible-book-value ratio of 1 or $5.9 per share. Potential share dilution and lower earnings outlook posed a 20–30 percent downside for Regions stock at 10× normalized earnings or 3× pre-provision earnings.

How Did It Play Out?

Regions Financial stock fell nearly 40 percent after S&P downgraded the U.S. AAA ratings on August 5, 2011. The stock continued to trade around $4 per share as Regions failed to sell Morgan Keegan to Stifel Financial in 2011. On March 13, 2012, Regions announced a public offering of approximately $900 million of its shares toward the plan to repurchase its $3.5 billion in TARP-preferred stocks. On April 2, 2012, it sold Morgan Keegan for $1.2 billion to Raymond James Financial.

Passage of the Baton from Bernanke to Yellen

On October 9, 2013, Janet Yellen was officially nominated to replace Ben Bernanke as head of the Federal Reserve. As I began researching Janet Yellen, I stumbled upon an excellent blog from the *Washington Post* that listed all of her key academic papers.[7] In a 2004 paper that she coauthored with her husband George Akerlof, her concern with underutilization of labor and policy response to high unemployment was clear:

> Stabilization policy can significantly reduce average levels of unemployment by providing stimulus to demand in circumstances where unemployment is high but underutilization of labor and capital does little to lower inflation. A monetary policy that vigorously fights high unemployment should, however, also be complemented by a policy that equally vigorously fights inflation when it rises above a modest target level. The Federal Reserve Act thus wisely enunciated price stability and maximum employment as twin goals for monetary policy.[8]

The U.S. unemployment rate was still hovering over 7 percent and inflation did not seem to be a concern for the Federal Reserve. Janet Yellen's background as a labor economist seemed to signal that her first priority would be to bring down unemployment to normalized levels and maintain a dovish stance. In other words, the low interest rate could stay put for the foreseeable future and the Fed "put" could encourage the U.S. stock market to continue to rise.

Keeping an Eye on the Economic Calendar

Investors watch for some key economic indicators other than the Federal Reserve calendar to gauge the state and outlook of the economy and the signs of economic downturn. The periodic release dates for economic data are important catalysts for the market.

Leading economic indicators:

1. Average weekly hours, manufacturing
2. Average weekly initial claims for unemployment insurance
3. Building permits, new private housing units
4. Index of consumer expectations
5. Interest rate spread, 10-year Treasury bonds less federal funds
6. Manufacturers' new orders, consumer goods and materials
7. Manufacturers' new orders, nondefense capital goods

Coincident economic indicators:

1. Employees on nonagricultural payrolls
2. Personal income less transfer payments

3. Industrial production
4. Manufacturing and trade sales

Lagging economic indicators:

1. Average duration of unemployment
2. Inventories-to-sales ratio, manufacturing and trade
3. Labor cost per unit of output, manufacturing
4. Average prime rate
5. Commercial and industrial loans
6. Consumer installment credit to personal income ratio
7. Consumer price index for services
8. GDP/Real GDP

Other industry-specific indicators include the S&P Case-Shiller Index, Mortgage Bankers Association (MBA) Mortgage Application Survey, and pending home sales for housing stocks. Monthly automobile and truck unit sales and monthly retail sales are important indicators for consumer stocks. Closely watched commodities data releases include Energy Information Association (EIA) crude oil supply and weekly natural gas storage report.

Market Fear Indicators

The three commonly watched fear indicators are TED spread, VIX, and CDS (e.g., CDX, iTraxx, Sovereign CDS, single-name CDS). These indicators are negatively correlated to the market and investors gauge the indicators to engage in tactical shorting to hedge their long positions.

TED spread (the difference between interbank loan rates and the risk-free treasury rate) measures the fear of systemic banking issues. VIX is the measure of 30-day expected volatility in the

S&P 500. VIX crossed 80 during the Lehman crisis, implying that the S&P 50 could move 80 percent on an annualized basis. CDS is a measure of credit risk.

I have included some charts to show their negative correlation with the S&P 500. Aggregate money outflow for equities is also a closely watched indicator. Money outflow tends to have amplified impact on equities, especially in emerging markets with low liquidity. I have also included a chart to show the correlation of foreign institutional investor money flow with the S&P BSE Sensex, the Indian stock market index.

TED Spread

A sharp increase in LIBOR (London Interbank Offered Rate), a benchmark short-term interest rate, reflects high credit risk in the banking system. Investors tend to flock to Treasury securities amid fears of a banking crisis and push down the Treasury yields, further widening the TED spread (figure 5.3).

VIX

VIX is a measure of implied volatility of 30-day options on the S&P 500. VIX tends to trade between 10 and 20 during periods of complacence and shoots up during market worries. VIX hit an all-time high of ~90 in October 2008, after the Lehman Brothers collapse (figure 5.4).

Spanish Sovereign CDS Versus S&P 500

Figure 5.5 shows the correlation between the change in Spanish sovereign CDS and S&P during the Euro zone crisis in 2011 and 2012.

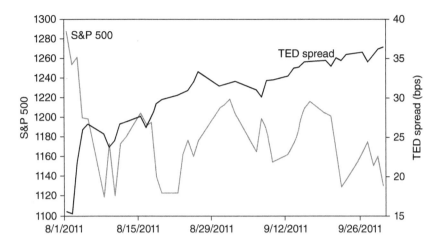

FIGURE 5.3 TED Spread vs. S&P 500, 2011 U.S. AAA downgrade. *Source:* Federal Reserve, S&P Dow Jones Indices.

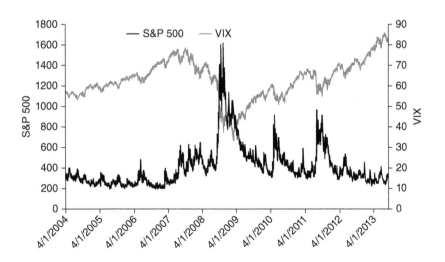

FIGURE 5.4 VIX vs. S&P 500. *Source:* Bloomberg, S&P Dow Jones Indices.

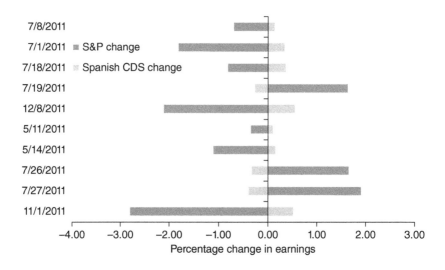

FIGURE 5.5 Negative correlation between Spanish sovereign CDS and S&P 500. *Source:* Bloomberg, S&P Dow Jones Indices.

Money Flows

Net monthly outflows of more than $2 billion can have a significant negative impact on the Indian stock market index.

Recap

- Comparison with the magnitude of past peak-to-trough corrections in the market can help to make sense of an ongoing crisis.
- Market behavior during a deepening crisis tends to rhyme. Look at history to understand if the crisis can balloon into a black swan event.
- Do not fight the Fed; they always have room to lend. Central banks can pump liquidity into the market for long periods of time.

- Predicting economic downturns to find short ideas is hard, but signs of tightening credit cycles can help to identify short ideas that are heavily dependent on credit markets.
- Economic data releases and market fear indicators can provide tactical trading ideas that are beyond the scope of this book.

PART II

How Successful Investors and Analysts Think

6

Value Investing

Plus ça change, plus c'est la même chose.
—JEAN-BAPTISTE ALPHONSE KARR

IN HIS INVESTMENT CLASSIC, *The Intelligent Investor*, Ben Graham made a clear distinction between investment and speculation: "An investment operation is one which, upon thorough analysis promises safety of principal and an adequate return. Operations not meeting these requirements are speculative."[1] When Ben Graham published this book in 1949, he had spent twenty-six years as a portfolio manager in his investment partnership and thirty-five years on Wall Street. He had seen it all about investing during these years, and there are no concepts on investing that escape his breadth of knowledge and experience. Investing is not any different today, even though Graham's book has reached the retirement age of 65.

Ben Graham: The Father of Value Investing

Ben Graham marked his foray into securities analysis with his bearish take on Missouri Pacific Railroad bonds in 1914. He was successful

in the ensuing fifteen years on Wall Street with almost any investment concepts touted by modern-day investors, such as his merger
arbitrage analysis of Guggenheim Exploration, hedging operations
with the purchase of convertible bonds and simultaneous short sale
of common stocks, participation in various Savold Tire initial public
offerings, the active short sale of overvalued stocks, and shareholder
activism with Northern Pipe Line. He did have an early tryst with
failure in 1917 as he suffered losses in the stocks that he bought on
margin—losses he had to repay over the next two years.

Graham's generosity in sharing his rich investing experience
and his decision to embark on a teaching career at Columbia University in 1928 became a boon for the later-generation investors.
It was the beginning of a new learning experience for Ben himself
as America fell into the Great Depression and his portfolio lost
nearly 70 percent. His losses stemmed in 1932 as he drew on
lessons from the crash to adjust his portfolio and wrote a series
of articles for *Forbes* titled, "Is American Business Worth More
Dead than Alive?" He also began working with David Dodd on
the investment textbook he had conceived six years earlier, which
would become an investment classic: *Security Analysis*.

Ben Graham on Value Investing and Short Selling

Ben Graham's emphasis on proper mental and emotional attitudes
toward investment decisions and knowing the difference between
the market price and the underlying value of securities are the
underpinnings of his value investing principles. He espoused
the idea of investing in public utility companies at their net-asset
value and reading the warning signs on growth companies, which
are in line with his businesslike approach to investing.

Graham regularly shorted overvalued stocks, although mostly
in the realm of an arbitrage or a hedging operation. He was not
shy to cut his losses in his rare naked short positions, as in the

case of Shattuck Corporation, a restaurant chain. In 1929, Ben Graham held $2.5 million of short positions as a hedge to his $4.5 million long positions; his shorts served him well as he closed them for a record profit after the market crash.

Graham made a clear distinction between value investing and short selling, as he pointed out in *The Intelligent Investor*. He also warned that analysts and investors must be wary to sell good companies short:

> Buying a neglected and therefore undervalued issue for profit generally proves a protracted and patience-trying experience. And selling short a too popular and therefore overvalued issue is apt to be a test not only of one's courage and stamina but also of the depth of one's pocketbook.

Short selling did not fit Graham's definition of investments but rather qualified as mostly a speculative or trading operation. Ben Graham minced no words in suggesting that it was reckless for an average public investor to engage in short selling. Short selling exposes the investor to the vagaries and fluctuations of the stock market and is at odds with value investing, which seeks to insulate the investor. Value investors would sell stocks to raise the cash levels of their portfolios to express their bearish opinions.

Ben Graham's genius was not limited to stocks. His breadth of knowledge extended to English, philosophy, drama, and mathematics, among many other subjects. Irvin Kahn, one of his early disciples, provided a great biographical account of Ben Graham in a 1977 paper written with Robert Milne.

The purpose of this chapter is not to reinvent the wheel of value investing but to highlight the time-tested nuggets of value investing wisdom from Ben Graham and the superinvestors of Graham and Doddsville led by Warren Buffett—a legendary investor and protégé of Ben Graham. *Intelligent Investor* emphasized three important value investing concepts, among many others.

Mr. Market, Price Versus Value, and Margin of Safety

Ben Graham's dissemination of these three concepts are at the core of value investing espoused by him. Stock portfolio fluctuations are almost a guarantee for any investor, and the only two possible ways for the investor to benefit from these fluctuations are *the way of timing* and *the way of pricing*. Graham pointed out the behavioral issue with the way of timing is that the speculator usually wants to make his profit in a hurry. In contrast, a serious investor does not expect to benefit from day-to-day fluctuations.

Mr. Market, the fabled character, changes his mind every day on the price of stocks; he is also subject to wild mood swings that can result in large fluctuations. Graham distilled his years of experience into this parable to point out that an intelligent investor's strength lies in his independent judgment to buy wisely when prices fall sharply and to sell wisely when they run up. The way of pricing puts the investor in the shoes of a business owner, putting the focus on the intrinsic value of the business; timing is not important unless it allows the investor to buy stocks below intrinsic value.

The investor can determine a sound purchase price at a discount to intrinsic value by applying the concept of margin of safety based on the stock's earning power or value of asset. Here, Graham made the important observation that investors lose money mostly from purchasing poor-quality businesses during favorable business cycles as opposed to purchasing high-quality stocks at high prices. Warren Buffett and his longtime business partner, Charlie Munger, have further expounded the idea of high-quality businesses in their numerous letters and interviews; in their view, businesses with a moat around them pose significant barriers to entry, such as brand strength, customer captivity, regulatory protection, and inimitable products.

An investor's ability to generate superior returns lies not only in behavioral strengths but also in the ability to understand business models and estimate the intrinsic values of businesses. Buffett and Munger tend to stick to their circle of competence. They have repeatedly advised investors to build and expand own their circle of competence in companies and industries that they find easy to understand.[2]

Value Investing Versus Short Selling

While *the way of pricing* constitutes the fabric of value investing and *the way of timing* is merely a supplementary consideration, *the way of timing* takes precedence for a short seller due to the short duration and complications arising from stock loans in short trades. Short selling is a speculative operation because it has an asymmetric risk profile, with its success depending on the prediction of stock moves, benevolence of stock lenders, and moods of the market. As Charlie Munger quipped in an interview with CNBC anchor Becky Quick on short selling, "We don't like trading agony for money."

Buffett explained Charlie's rationale:

The reason he said that is because a stock, when you short it, can theoretically go to infinity. When you buy a stock at 10, you can only lose 10 points. When you short a stock at 10, it can go to 100 or 200. And occasionally you'll get into a situation on a short where you may know eventually it's going to turn out to be worth nothing, or very close to it, or it's a fraud, but what it can do in between can be very, very unpleasant. We like to sleep well, and you can't sleep well if you're short a lot of stocks.

These legendary investors have repeatedly warned about the fallacies of short selling.

Seth Klarman also pointed out two key practical constraints on short selling in his out-of-print classic, *Margin of Safety*: restrictive short-sale rules that can cause stocks to remain overvalued, and the limited number of short sellers because most institutional investors are prohibited from short selling. Klarman echoed Buffett and Munger's concerns with short selling: "A conservative investor may not feel comfortable with a professional short-seller no matter how favorable the results."

What Motivates Hedge Funds to Engage in This Inherently Risky Practice?

The meat of the incentive structures of hedge funds is in profit sharing and their goal to deliver absolute returns regardless of the market conditions. Now, delivering absolute returns in a bear market is impossible without a short-selling product for hedge funds. How else can they "hedge" the downside risk in a bear market, after all? Their clients are willing to share part of their profit in return for the hope of an absolute return.

As we can see in table 6.1, hedge funds will earn twice as much as long-only funds, even if both of them generate an average return of 10 percent per year for 5 years (not compounded). Now, if these 5 years turn out to be the best bull market and the returns go up from 10 to 15 percent, hedge funds will earn 3.5 times as much as their long-only peers. Conversely, if these 5 years are a mixed bag of bull and bear markets and the returns end up negative, hedge funds will still earn at least as much as their long-only peers.

If Value Investors Are Reluctant to Short Sell, How Do They Hedge Risks?

Seth Klarman stands tall among modern-day value investors, and he is intensely focused on risk. His approach to hedging portfolio

Table 6.1
Management fees for similar-sized hedge funds and long-only funds

	Hedge funds	Long-only funds
Assets under management ($ millions)	1,000	1,000
Management fees (at 2% for 5 years)	$100 million	$100 million
10% annual returns (not compounded)	20% profit share	0% profit share
Year 1	$20 million	0
Year 2	$20 million	0
Year 3	$20 million	0
Year 4	$20 million	0
Year 5	$20 million	0
Total management fees	$200 million	$100 million

risks is not at odds with the intelligent investor approach because he eliminates the asymmetric risk profile and short duration nature of short trades. Simply put, his approach is akin to buying insurance for 5 years, where the payoff can be many times greater than the premiums in the event of an expected or unexpected crisis. Klarman's small portfolio allocations in long-term insurance instruments, such as long-term equity anticipation securities and credit default swaps, have more than compensated for any portfolio losses during black swan events.

An Interview with a Value Investor

Jean-Marie Eveillard is a reputed value investor who employed a diversified approach to portfolio management while he ran First Eagle Global Fund from 1979 to 2004. He took a two-pronged approach to hedging systemic risks—raising the cash allocation in the portfolio when there were no compelling opportunities and buying gold as a form of portfolio insurance against market panics. The fund returned approximately 16 percent on an annual basis (or cumulative 44× returns over those twenty-five years).

I first met Jean-Marie at Columbia Business School, where he was a regular guest on investment panels and value investing classes. I was later formally introduced to him by one of his protégés at First Eagle.

Morningstar, Inc. presented its first Fund Manager Lifetime Achievement Award to Jean-Marie in 2003. In 2007, *Fortune* magazine named him one of Wall Street's best value investors. First Eagle Global Fund had approximately 16 percent average annual returns during his twenty-six years at the helm. During these years, he stayed true to the value investing philosophy and a diversified investing style. Here, I interview Jean-Marie on his methods as a value investor.

Q: Let us begin with your early years at Société Générale. How did you convince them to venture into value investing?

I did not convince them. Gee, I wasted the first fifteen years of my professional life. It was not until 1968 that I was first exposed to Graham and the idea of value investing. In [the] summer of '1968, I met two Frenchmen at Columbia University and we used to cycle in central park. They told me about Ben Graham and about his classic, *The Intelligent Investor*. I was more interested in *The Intelligent Investor* than in Ben Graham's other book on security analysis.

So, I did not find an investment style during my first five years and then the French bank did not let me venture into value investing in the ensuing ten years. Their own style was to trade in and out of the big stocks in the index; basically, they were closet index huggers. In late 1978, I came back to New York and heard Lee Cooperman talk about Warren Buffet very positively. I had to order physical copies of Berkshire's annual reports for the last ten years because, remember, this was not the Internet era. I discovered Warren Buffett and how he made successful adjustments to the teaching of Ben Graham. As luck would have it, the bank sent me back to New York to run SoGen International Fund, a $15 million fund that was subcontracted to Smith Barney. I had full discretion over the fund and I worked alone—without even a salesman—for seven years until 1986.

In 1970, Société Générale did not want to do an offshore fund because there had been a big offshore scandal in [the 1960s] involving Bernie Cornfeld's Investors Overseas Services. Now, if you only had a SEC [Security and Exchange Commission] registered fund, you could sell the fund in the United States but not in France. Société Générale had strong distribution in France but it could not sell my fund in France, and consequently, my fund did not grow from 1970 to 1978. Meanwhile, SEC called me to Washington in 1986 because they wanted to close my fund down due to a mistake in our Net Asset Value (NAV). We had subcontracted our accounting work but SEC wanted to hold us accountable for a five-cent discrepancy over the accounting treatment of accrued interests on some of the bonds we had sold. Ultimately, we got away with just a SEC warning.

There is a story about Napoleon: his entourage surrounds him when one of his aides says that a certain general is lazy. Napoleon retorted that the general had done well in the last battle, to which the aide replied that the general just got lucky. Napoleon said, "Did you say lucky? I want lucky generals." So, I too was lucky.

Q: Could you contrast Buffett's approach to that of Graham?

Warren Buffett's approach to value investing is more time consuming than Graham's approach. As you have mentioned in this chapter, Ben Graham often talked about high-quality businesses, but he is known more for his deep value investing style. Buffett introduced more of the qualitative elements of value investing analysis.

The [19]70s were difficult for the stock market and it did not become easy to find Ben Graham–type stocks until the early [19]80s (i.e., deep value stocks). In [the] late [19]90s, I suffered because I refused to participate in the telecom boom stocks where there was absolutely no value. As a result, I lagged from 1997 to 1999 and our fund assets went down from 6 billion to nearly 2 billion, even though we were still making money.

Q: Why did the investors start pulling money?

When you lag on the market for six to twelve months, the investors begin to leave, and then they completely desert you if you continue to lag on the market for more than two years. Conversely, the investors do not start believing in your performance until you have a good run for one year. When I reflect back on this period, I find it painful because the board of directors turned against me and they decided in Paris to sell the investment advisory firm. They still did not fire me, however. John Arnold was either lucky or smart to acquire us at a really cheap price at that time. Eventually, the technology bubble burst in March of 2000. Inflows in my funds started after a hiatus of one year.

Q: So you never really convinced Société Générale about value investing?

I never managed to convince them. I performed well from 1979 to 1996; however, the board of directors never understood my style and always remained suspicious. While my value strategy worked, they always expected it to stop working at some point. Jeremy Grantham says that most of [the] "sell" side only has a six- to twelve-month view of a business. But, to look at the business with six- to twelve-month period in mind is a completely different approach than looking at it over five years.

Q: Would you consider your investment style closer to Ben Graham or Warren Buffett? Can you also describe your approach to value investing and the reason behind your emphasis the importance of balance sheet?

I started with [a] Ben Graham approach because I was working alone and Graham's approach was more quantitative than qualitative, [and] hence easier. We eventually moved closer to [a] Buffett approach as we began to hire analysts in the [19]90s. Today, with the exception of Japan and micro-cap stocks, there are really no Ben Graham type stocks to find. There are no hostile takeovers in Japan, so the Japanese companies are under no pressure to allocate their capital wisely. Ben Graham did speak about high-quality businesses, but Buffett and Munger actually focused more closely on high-quality businesses. Graham's approach is less time consuming and easier if you know the numbers and if you are careful to read footnotes.

When everyone and their brethren were buying Enron, someone at our firm asked, "Why don't we own Enron?" We looked at Enron and one of my analysts found that one of their footnotes was incomprehensible. When we called the Enron CEO [chief financial officer] and his lieutenants, they were evasive in explaining the footnote. We threw the Enron investor material in the trash and moved on because we were not satisfied with that one footnote. You can understand the significance of balance sheet in the case of Enron.

A friend of mine once said accounting reflects the mind of the people. For example, German firms tend to point out every risk associated with their business—risks which are sometimes hard to imagine. I had always wondered why the U.S. has not privatized JFK and LaGuardia airports while the U.K. has privatized its airports. We checked the accounting assumptions for runway depreciation for the private airports. British airports depreciated their runways over a hundred years while Copenhagen depreciated their runways over thirty years. When you make the comparison, you can see two ends of the spectrum: too aggressive versus too conservative accounting.

I do not like companies with low effective tax rates (except for countries like Hong Kong with natural low tax rates), because either the companies are trying to cheat the tax authorities or they have fancy accounting and the companies are not making much money. Their earnings quality will often turn out to be poor.

The Buffett approach implies the exercise of judgment in addition to looking at accounting, which admittedly, every now and then, can also lead to erroneous judgment. I helped someone teach a value investing course at Columbia and I told the students that I don't want a forty-five page paper on a stock. We don't need to know everything about the company, but instead we want to know the major strengths and weaknesses of the company. This can easily be summarized and produced in a four- to five-page paper. Yes, you run the risk of missing something important, but that is how you can build upon exercising your judgment. We will not blame you in that case. I mean, I have been wrong in many cases.

Q: Can you talk about an example of your approach to analyze the strengths and weaknesses of a business?

About twenty years ago, someone mentioned to me that David Swenson had started buying timberland. I said, let me look at timberland, which was a great business in my view. Weyerhaeuser had acquired most of the timberlands a hundred years ago for $1 per acre while the prevailing prices were $3,000–$4,000 per acre. So, the balance sheet values were misleading and you needed to make adjustments to both assets and liabilities. In those days, engineers who liked shiny and expensive paper machines ran paper and pulp companies. As a result, the tremendous cash flow generated by timber business was dissipated in processing timber into pulp and paper. Over a full business cycle, the investment returns were mediocre at best. David Swensen was not buying the stocks. Instead, he bought the physical timberlands. We decided to wait on buying the stocks as well.

Plum Creek and Rayonier were among the companies that divested most of the wood processing businesses within a radius of fifteen miles from Seattle. Pope Resources was spun off from Pope and Talbot. Interestingly, three to five years later in the [19]80s, Pope and Talbot went bankrupt. They could no longer generate cash through the timber business to subsidize the processing businesses. So, there was only one thing to know in this case: the quality of timber business and that processing business is highly cyclical and capital intensive.

Q: So, which business qualities/characteristics do you find to work more in the realm of Buffett's style of investing?

Buffett likes businesses with sustainable competitive advantages. For example, he likes the brick business because you cannot transport bricks too far because then they will lose their competitive edge. Quarries are similar businesses—no one wants a quarry in their backyard. Some of quarries have a life of 75–100 years. Most of these businesses have sustainable local competitive advantages.

Sometimes, the firm's management is the differentiator. For instance, let me talk about Sodexo, a French catering business with 300,000 people. There were only three worldwide companies. Compass in Britain and Aramark in [the United States] were the other companies. Someone once told me, "Retail is detail." There was plenty of detail in Sodexo to look at. Their voucher business within catering was very profitable. After the Second World War,

Sodexo was one of the growth companies on the Paris exchange. However, the founder never got along with investors because he didn't like what the portfolio managers and analysts wanted him to do with his business in the short term. He was focused on the long term and he said that, though he was mortal, if he took care of his business, it would outlive him. Their British subsidiary was not doing well and portfolio managers used to point to Compass, which had higher return on equity. It later turned out that Compass had been using creative accounting to cover up.

Sometimes, companies in the U.S. and U.K. follow accounting practices that observe the letter of the law but betray the spirit of law. In contrast, in continental Europe (i.e., France and Germany), it is not as easy to betray the spirit of law because according to the law, everything that is not specifically authorized is forbidden. Before Compass admitted to loose accounting, the financial community turned against Sodexo and its stock fell. We bought some Sodexo stock at this point because we believed the management was focused on the long term.

The founder also could see that we were long-term investors. Chuck, one of our analysts who later left to start IVA [International Value Advisors], used to cover the company. He got along well with the founder. He was invited by Sodexo to come to their New Jersey headquarters to speak to its U.S. executives about our investment approach because they believed that our approach to long-term investing was in line with that of their own.

Q: When do you decide to sell a stock?

We made mistakes with Swissair in [the 1990s] that would indirectly answer your question on when to sell the stock. I looked at Swissair from Ben Graham standpoint but I misread the impact of leverage. When you look at things from a Graham perspective you have to be extremely careful about leverage. For example, if you estimate the value of assets to be 100 and debt is 70, the equity is worth 30. If you are wrong by 10 percent on the asset value (which is not difficult) and the value turns out to be 90, the equity is now worth only 20. The value of equity is now 33 percent lower. As the saying goes, asset values are contingent but debt is forever.

From a high-quality standpoint, we found that Swissair had all sorts of good subsidiaries— hotels and an extremely profitable business in Turkey. Their nickname was "flying bank" because they were a cash machine with no leverage. They had a young fleet and very good reputation for service. Originally, from a deep value standpoint, Swissair was depreciating the fleet quickly.

They made a mistake that I did not realize immediately. They hired a consultant as their CEO [chief executive officer]. He began to make big plans to make Swissair a global airline by acquiring Belgian Airlines, which turned out to be a fiasco. I was very slow to react to this news. One should be quick to sell if things turn sour or one is worried that the business model appears to be changing for the worse. Sometimes, such a change to business model can result from outside forces. For example, some American newspapers started failing with the advent of the internet. This was not necessarily because of the complete failings of their management, but rather because they did not charge for newspaper online quickly enough.

So after some time, I realized that [the] Swissair CEO was not doing good things for the business. In such a case, one should be quick to sell the stock, acknowledge the mistake to avoid a permanent loss of capital, and move on to something else. Conversely, one should be very slow to sell if the company appears to have [a] competitive advantage.

Q: There is a group of ardent Buffett followers who do not believe in selling the stock. What are your views on that?

Several weeks back, Bruce Greenwald pointed out to me that Buffett never sells. There are two reasons: firstly, Buffett makes few mistakes. He once acquired a shoe business and was quick to get out because it did not work and he got out of some oil stocks as well. Secondly, if you think you are holding on to a business with strong moat around it and it trades close to, or slightly above, its intrinsic value, you have to come up with another business with a real moat to replace your original investment. Now, the problem becomes graver when the stock becomes very overvalued. Buffett himself acknowledged that he should have sold some Coca-Cola in 1997, when Coke stock seemed vastly overvalued.

If the business begins to deteriorate and stock is modestly over-valued, the stock can fall a lot very quickly. You have to be quick to determine if the weakness is temporary or not. Marty Whitman says if the weakness is temporary, then the losses are temporary and unrealized as well. Now, only time can tell whether you can call it temporary unrealized losses or permanent loss of capital. I personally have tried to be slow in selling unusual businesses from [a] quality standpoint. With the exception of Swissair, I am quick to sell businesses where I think the business model has changed for the worse.

Q: As a value investor, you do not believe in short selling. Can you talk about some of behavioral reasons that prevent value investors from engaging in short selling?

Some mutual funds that specify in their prospectus that they short sell can do so, but we do not engage in short selling. You gave the perfect answer earlier in this chapter when you quote Charlie Munger that he doesn't trade agony for money. Buffett says the loss can be unlimited and even if a company turns out to be a fraud, it can take a long time for the market to discover the fraud. Short selling can be a very painful experience. Instead, increasing cash allocation is a good alternative to short selling for value investors.

Most mutual funds say they have to be fully invested, unlike our funds. They fear to antagonize their intermediaries, financial planners, and brokers who will tell them that they are not paid to hold cash. This is nonsense. Their prospectuses might say they have to be a 100 percent in cash but there may not necessarily be a regulatory compulsion to stay fully invested. In our case, we have 1 million shareholders. The idea that the investor is not paying the manager to hold cash is erroneous. Investors pay shareholder advisory fees and give money to portfolio managers in order to do good work over the long term. If I have enough investment ideas, then I will keep only a modest amount of cash for redemption. However, if I don't have enough ideas, I will keep more cash. Some might argue that I should increase the position size of the stocks I own. But that would not make sense if the stock has moved up and I am not trying to time the market. In general, cash is an important tool for the value investors.

Q: What do you think about the role of a short seller in the stock market?

They have a very legitimate role in the stock market as long as they don't propagate rumors. Many value investors are reluctant to accept short sellers as part of the stock market. I believe that some short sellers have been good at identifying fraud and they should be complimented for that. The fact that short sellers exist and they can practice their art successfully keeps some people—especially management—on their guard. As long as short sellers behave within the confines of the law, they are very valuable to the stock market.

Q: You have relied on changing cash allocation in the portfolio to shield from downturns. Is keeping cash a way for a long-only value investor to express a short opinion?

In more than 50 years of my investing career, I have seen only one incidence in the late [19]80s where I could barely own one stock in an entire geography (i.e., Japan). I had looked at forty-five stocks and I could not own more than one because the entire market was a joke. In 1988, I sold my last Japanese stock and the stock market moved another 30 percent. Briefly, the Tokyo stock market was the largest stock market in the world. We were bearish and we kept cash.

Financial brokers will call me and say it is one thing to be underweight [in] Japanese markets, but it is preposterous to not own anything in the second largest stock market in the world. I would tell them that I owned nothing because I have not been able to find a single stock that I would like to own. They would point out stocks trading at 45× P/E stocks that were trading at discount to the stock market that was trading at 60× P/E. I would chuckle. It was not until the 1990s that I saw a similar situation in the U.S. markets. However, there was a clear divide between new economy and old economy stocks. In this situation, we had plenty of choices in the U.S. old economy stocks.

Q: Bob Rodriguez of First Pacific Advisors had a similar style as yours. For long-value investors, is there another way to be short?

Yes. They can also buy cheap credit default swap (CDS)-like instruments, as Seth Klarman has done in the past from the standpoint of portfolio insurance. But Seth can do things similar to hedge funds that ordinary mutual funds cannot. I don't think we can buy CDS because it is a derivative. We do not participate in derivatives.

Seth Klarman can also buy out of the money "call and put" options. When I was at the wedding of Jim Grant's daughter, Seth and I were at the same table. He told me that he has two advantages over other funds. One, he was a value investor, and two, his investors think along the same line as him. He doesn't worry about redemption. He started out with family offices and his funds remained closed to outside investors most of the time. When he would reopen, he would selectively decide his investors. He could easily say no to a fund from a funds investor who may have a short-term orientation. In my next life, I would probably like to run a closed-end fund.

Q: How important is it for value investors to pay attention to overall macroeconomic conditions and market levels? Have you paid attention to the macro in the past?

Value investors are normally bottom-up investors and do not believe as much in paying attention to the macro. I am familiar with [the] Austrian school of economics, where they talk about credit boom and bust. Every boom is followed by [a] bust, just like the night follows the day. I like the emphasis they place on credit cycles because credit booms end badly, and I like their analysis of the 1920s. There is a famous anecdote about a professor at an Austrian school, who had just got engaged and also got an offer at a large bank. His fiancée wanted him to take the offer and quit professorship for the money. He replied that the last place he wanted to join is a bank. Indeed, the bank went kaput in 1930.

In the late [19]80s, with the appearance of leveraged buyouts (LBO), I asked myself if this was the beginning of a credit boom. Rupert Murdoch of News Corp was very much in debt and so was Sam Zell. They only escaped because the credit boom reappeared. Alan Greenspan, when he flooded liquidity in the market in 1987, caused problems to disappear quickly. With his success with the 1987 problem related to portfolio insurance, Greenspan became motivated to flood liquidity in response to any, and every, other problem as well.

In the case of News Corp, it is important to understand that banks cannot easily force people into bankruptcy and they also don't like to force bankruptcies. News Corp had issued bonds in all sorts of currencies. Swiss banks were desirous to compete with Wall Street funds and they had also issued papers for News Corp in these currencies. When the investment banks were reluctant to distribute, Swiss Banks had stuffed their own clients with these bonds. The problem was that these bonds were now trading at sixty-five cents on a dollar. They didn't want to mark the discount, especially right after the bonds were issued at par.

We bought these junk bonds in 1990 because these bonds provided equity-type returns. If the company doesn't go bankrupt until the bond goes par, you can make a lot of money—almost an equity-type double-digit return for holding bonds. In the case of bonds, the company either needs to have cash flow to service their debt or needs to have assets in excess of the debt. News Corp had a temporary cash flow problem but they had asset protection. A corporation, if it can avoid bankruptcy, will avoid the bankruptcy at any cost because bankruptcy is an acceptance of failure. In contrast to corporate bonds, sovereign bonds entail the risk of not only a sovereign country's ability to service the debt but also its willingness to service the debt.

I started worrying about [a] credit boom in 1980s, which interrupted briefly before resuming again at the beginning of the century. It accelerated in real estate and the music didn't stop until the last guy with no assets, no income, and no cash flow was able to get credit with no money down. My worry about the credit boom motivated me to raise cash levels and buy gold during the 2008 financial crisis, and we declined 21 percent when most value investors had declined by over 40 percent or worse.

I should have been much more demanding about the valuation in 2008 because I knew something bad was going to happen. I didn't have enough cash. The bottom-up investor didn't listen to the top-down investor in me.

Q: As the Federal Reserve begins to taper bond purchases and consider raising rates, how should value investors prepare for a possible impact on valuation multiples in the market?

The Federal Reserve and United States Congress have taken unprecedented steps in the wake of the financial crisis of 2008.

As a result, we are in an undefined period and it is a new economic landscape, possibly. However, there will be more recessions and the economy will grow again consequently. I have the same kind of worries about the economy as I had during the crisis. We are very demanding on valuation right now about buying new stocks in our portfolio and there is no better time to focus on diversification.

Seth is paying attention to the macro and he is worried about what will happen to the economy. I share the same worries about valuation. My successor shares the same belief. I don't know if it is too early to raise more cash, but it is time to be more demanding about valuation because I don't know if we are in the same economic landscape anymore. Whenever Ben Graham was asked about the expectations, he said the future was uncertain. He said, "Look, intrinsic value is important but things can happen and there is a need for diversification."

Q: You have often spoken about gold as calamity insurance as well as an inflation hedge. You have been critical of the Neo-Keynesian policies and believe that gold is also a hedge against failures of Keynesian policies.

Today, people believe financial crises are a thing of past—low risk of inflation, low risk of financial crisis. The steps taken by central banks and the U.S. Congress in terms of increase in public debt and deficit are unprecedented. This is the biggest crisis since the Great Depression, possibly threatening a new economic landscape. Value investors were historically helped by recessions because they bought on the way down and sold on the way up. Many value investors took the attitude to spend no time on the top-down because they like to buy on the way down. Value investors were caught unaware. They didn't realize that the profits for financial services, banks in particular, were fictitious. For two years, they made money. William White, the chief economist for Bank of

International Settlement (BIS), wrote a paper that low inflation was not enough and talked about longer-term consequences of asset price bubbles and financial imbalances in the setting of current interest rates. He talked about the role of monetary policy in a Keynesian macroeconomic model in which financial imbalances play a role and where their subsequent unwinding may lead to a credit crunch or similar financial distress. The paper was interesting but I didn't know when the bad times would arrive. We believe that buying gold is buying insurance against such bad times.

Q: You mentioned that you owned BIS stocks. Why did BIS sell their stock to private investors and not central banks and sovereigns?

Isolationists in the United States Senate did not want the [United States] to be a shareholder in an organization that was dominated by a majority of Europeans. The American tranche that was reserved for Americans was sold to the public, and so was the Belgian tranche because they refused to participate. We took ownership in 1980s because the BIS were self-satisfied bureaucrats. We looked at BIS stock as a combination of gold bullion and [a] money market fund. BIS owned gold bullions because the bank was capitalized with gold bullion at the time of creation and money market funds because 90 percent of the assets and liabilities would typically mature within a year.

So, BIS would invest liabilities such as deposits from Central Banks in J.P. Morgan short-term paper. BIS stock was trading at 40–50 percent discount to the NAV adjusted for the price of gold. A French economist told me that he was visiting BIS and asked me if I had any questions for them. I was curious about a provision in their liabilities. The answer I received was that it was a provision for a highly unlikely event and it was equity for all good purposes. We hoped that BIS didn't sell the gold and that they would continue to increase the dividends. Shortly after the turn of the century, when the IMF [International Monetary Fund] was discredited due to emerging markets crisis and World Bank loans were alleged to have ended up in the wrong pockets in Africa, I suspect, BIS believed they had a chance to become a major multinational institution that could displace World Bank and IMF in charge of preventing future financial crises. They did not want public shareholders anymore.

Recap

- According to Ben Graham, "An investment operation is one which, upon thorough analysis promises safety of principal and an adequate return. Operations not meeting these requirements are speculative."[3]
- There are three core concepts for value investing—price versus value, Mr. Market, and margin of safety.
- The way of pricing puts the investor in the shoes of a business owner, putting the focus on the intrinsic value of the business. Timing is not important unless it allows the investor to buy stocks below intrinsic value.
- Mr. Market, the fabled character, changes his mind every day on the price of stocks, and he is also subject to wild mood swings that can result in large fluctuations and create opportunities.
- The investor can determine a sound purchase price at a discount to intrinsic value by applying the concept of margin of safety based on the stock's earning power or value of asset.

Key Takeaways from the Interview with Jean-Marie Eveillard

- When you lag on the market for six to twelve months, the investors begin to leave and then they completely desert you if you continue to lag on the market for more than two years. Conversely, the investors do not start believing in your performance until you have a good run for one year.

- If the business begins to deteriorate and stock is modestly overvalued, the stock can fall a lot very quickly. You have to be quick to determine if the weakness is temporary or not.
- One should be quick to sell the stock, acknowledge the mistake to avoid a permanent loss of capital, and move on to something else.
- Conversely, one should be very slow to sell if the company appears to have a competitive advantage.
- In general, cash is an important tool for the value investor.

7

Activist Investing

Shareholder activism won't go away and scares the hell out of
all of our managers.
—WARREN BUFFET

THIRTY YEARS AFTER BEN GRAHAM tried shareholder activism
with Northern Pipelines, Warren Buffett (Graham's protégé) had
his first tryst with shareholder activism. In the 1950s, Buffett took
a large stake in Sanborn Map and forced the company to separate
its investment portfolio from its core business. Sanborn stock had
been trading significantly below the value of its investments and
management had not exhibited interest in closing the gap.

In the 1960s, Buffett acquired a large stake in Berkshire Hathaway, then a textile business, and he received a verbal agreement
for a tender offer of $11.5 per share. Buffett felt slighted when
Berkshire tried to shortchange him by offering $11.375 per share.
He bought the entire company and fired the chief executive officer
(CEO). Berkshire's textile business kept dying and Buffett admitted that he made a mistake by buying Berkshire.

His stance on activist investing changed over the next few years
when he bought nearly ten percent of *Washington Post* in 1973.
Warren Buffett reached out to Katherine Graham and pacified her
concerns about his stake. They became friends and Buffett joined

Washington Post's board. Warren Buffett has since engaged in friendly acquisitions.

However, the 1980s saw the rise of corporate raiders as leveraged buyouts (LBOs) flourished, marking the beginning of the credit boom. This era is famously portrayed in some iconic scenes of the movies *Wall Street* and *Barbarians at the Gate*. Some executives of the targeted conglomerates were forced to break up their companies to unlock value, while others fended off raiders by introducing poison pills (issuing more stocks and diluting the raider's stake) and golden parachutes (extraordinary severance benefits in the event of a takeover). This era ended with the bankruptcy of Drexel, the investment bank involved in LBO financing, and it financed a number of mega deals including the maiden LBO of RJR Nabisco by KKR as well as Phillips 66 by Carl Ichan and MGM by Ted Turner.

Drexel was mired in illegal junk bond market dealings led by Michael Milken, and the bank was investigated by multiple U.S. regulators, threatening it with indictment under RICO (the Racketeer Influenced and Corrupt Organizations Act). While Drexel was able to settle the charges, it was faced with the collapse of the junk bond market when the LBO of United Airlines fell through on Oct 13, 1989. Drexel was forced into bankruptcy and the booming LBO market came to a halt. Some corporate raiders from the LBO era morphed their role over the next decade into activist investors.

A new generation of activist investors also arrived on the scene at the turn of the twenty-first century. These investors buy stocks in undervalued companies and pressure company boards to unlock value by buying back shares, taking steps to improve operating profits, or shaking out management ranks. In general, when an activist investor gets involved, the target stocks tend to rise because of the successful track record of the activist. Short sellers in such companies face headwinds from a push by the activist to introduce changes in favor of the stock.[1]

An Interview with Bill Ackman

Bill Ackman is a uniquely successful activist investor who has not only pushed for changes through his long investments but also shined a spotlight on troubled companies through his activist short positions. His prolonged battle with MBIA as a result of his short position in the company is captured in the book *Confidence Game*. Eventually, Bill was proven correct, and he stuck to his guns on his short thesis on MBIA for six years. Bill Ackman is a value investor as well; however, he takes a concentrated approach in his investments. He agreed to provide an interview for the book and share his insights on investing here.

Q: Can you talk about accounting and liquidity considerations in your public equity investments today?

During my first two years of employment, I worked for a real estate service firm that arranged financing for developers. I saw some successful and unsuccessful investors in real estate. The smart ones did not care about GAAP [generally accepted accounting principles] but used cash flow to assess value. Accounting is an imprecise language. How much cash a business generates over its life will determine its value, so learning how to translate GAAP accounting to economic earnings was an important learning for me.

What is remarkable about the public markets is the ability with minimal frictional cost to buy and sell securities even at an enormous scale. The option to abandon a good investment for a better one is a great aspect of the public markets. If you take a company private by buying 100 percent of the equity, you cannot buy more of it. In the public markets, every one of your holdings is priced every day, and you can add more to your position and vice versa. You don't need to hire an investment bank to sell your company. The ability to switch seats is a very valuable one.

Q: How do you find the research approach to find long invest- ments different from that of short investments?

I find [the] Graham and Buffett approach about margin of safety (i.e., a wide spread between the price you pay and value) to be a very useful construct. We concentrate our capital in a handful of high-quality businesses. We prefer simple, predictable, free-cash-flow-generative businesses with dominant characteristics, which Buffett describes as companies with moats around them. We look for stock prices that allow one to buy a business at a significant discount to its intrinsic value as is, and at an even greater discount if the business can be optimized. We look to understand the fac- tors that cause these discounts, factors that we can influence by being a shareholder in the company. If we believe we can catalyze the necessary changes, and the discount to intrinsic value is large enough, we invest. That's the long approach.

The short approach is equivalent in some sense—the analogy to a margin of safety is what we call a "ceiling on valuation." By "ceiling on valuation," we mean an estimate of the reasonable worst-case outcome if the market were to ignore our negative views on a company. There are some businesses where it is easier to determine a ceiling on valuation than others. If you are shorting an internet-based business model with rapidly growing revenues without any cash generation, the stock market can assign an extremely high valuation without any meaningful upward-bound growth because it is difficult to precisely value this kind of high-growth business. You can short the stock and it can double or triple from there because the value is tied to hopes and dreams.

We don't short those types of companies; in fact, we short very few stocks at all. We have shorted a handful of stocks over the twelve-year history of the firm because of the inherent risk-reward equation (i.e., downside is unlimited). Short selling can be much more treacherous on the downside. We look for cases where a business can disappear (e.g., financial institutions with inadequate reserves that can be deemed insolvent by regulators or the market). We also look for companies that are violating the law—Herbalife violating the anti-pyramid and anti-deceptive marketing laws of the FTC [Federal Trade Commission]. We look for cases where a company is violating securities laws; cases where regulators will take down the company.

Q: Can you explain some of the inefficiencies in corporations that lend to your style of investing activism?

Companies for which cost control, strategy change, management change, better allocation of capital, monetizing hidden assets, or helping the market rethink the nature of the business can contribute meaningfully to unlocking value.

Q: When you started in the business, what caused you to pursue an activist investing style?

It is probably my personality and my frustration with being a passive investor when I see a huge opportunity that is not exploited by a company. It is a large competitive advantage to not be limited to the status quo in selecting investments.

Q: Can you talk about your capital allocation approach, position sizes, and how you manage risk at a portfolio level?

We manage risk first by not using margin leverage. Margin leverage is a dangerous source of capital because you can be wiped out when the market crashes. Without margin leverage, we can afford to think about each investment as a stand-alone investment with particular risks and opportunities for rewards. We prefer large-cap North American companies that generate simple, predictable cash flows that have limited exposure to extrinsic factors we cannot control.

While nearly every company is exposed to GDP [gross domestic product], our companies are generally very stable businesses that will not be materially impaired by negative GDP growth. We do not like businesses where commodity prices can have a huge impact. Beyond investment selection, buying at a discounted price is one of our greatest risk-management devices.

Q: Is it true that you avoid leverage at the portfolio level, as well as pass-through leverage in your portfolio companies?

We generally prefer investment-grade companies, but they are rarely debt free. Occasionally, we have invested in highly leveraged companies. For example, General Growth Properties was highly leveraged, with $200 million in equity and $27 billion in debt. We sized our position smaller in General Growth for this reason.

Q: Could you talk about some of your past research that you consider to be your best?

General Growth is probably our best investment, not just because we made a fortune on the investment (i.e., a more than 130-fold return compared to the initial purchase cost and about 60 times our average cost), but also because our involvement enabled us to maximize value for all stakeholders.

General Growth stock would very likely have gone to zero had we not bought 25 percent of the company, convinced the board to file for Chapter 11, joined the board, and led a restructuring with creditors. We worked with management and the company's advisors to implement a restructuring that benefited all of the creditors—creditors got par plus accrued interest and shareholders have recovered nearly all of their investment. We brought in a new management team and came up with the idea of spinning off

Howard Hughes, which we executed. We hired a new management team for Howard Hughes and I currently chair the board. You could call it our magnum opus.

I think Herbalife on the short side rivals MBIA in the quality and level of research we have done. It has not yet been profitable. Herbalife has been levering up and buying the stock, which has propped up the stock, but the leverage is also putting them in a weaker position. Their buybacks will end in June 2015, so we will see then.

Q: Do you think it is inherently difficult to generate alpha on shorts than longs?

It is harder and creates more brain damage than you can imagine. Will we do it again? I will give the same answer I gave the last time. We waited five years after closing the MBIA short investment before we built our Herbalife position. We may wait another five, ten, or twenty years to do the next one. Who knows, we may never get involved in shorts in the future. If and when Herbalife plays out the way we expect, perhaps the next time we will just say the name of the company without taking a short position and wait for it to go to zero.

Q: What are your thoughts about short sellers and their role in the market?

Short sellers play a very important role in the market. Collectively, short sellers have a lot more resources than government regulators. They can devote a lot of time and attention to one company and do a lot of research to uncover frauds. That is a very helpful thing for the market. They can also help cushion volatility in the market as the buyer of last resort when stocks crash.

Q: Back to your sleep-at-night test: how do you handle stress?

I am an inherently stable, healthy, and resilient person and I am economically well-off. I also don't have 100 percent of my net worth invested in the funds. It is important in investing to not let volatility affect your judgment. It is easier to behave that way when all of your resources are not committed to your investment fund. It is better for your investors as well because people can act irrationally when they have too much of their capital in their fund. I have the vast majority of my liquid net worth in my fund, but I have enough outside that I can live without worrying about market volatility.

I don't find investing stressful because we do our homework and know what we own. Our portfolio is comprised of the highest quality businesses in the world, and we purchased these companies at attractive prices. This is inherently a relatively low-risk strategy.

Q: How do you remain confident throughout your trades, even when the market does not respond as you anticipate?

People and markets constantly judge you over short periods. In the Herbalife [trade], eighteen months into our short position, the stock is up 30 percent above where we shorted. It's noise. [*chuckles*] Stock markets can be wrong for a long time, but you have to be able to survive that period.

Q: You spotted a systemic issue with monolines before anyone else. Why did you decide to begin shorting MBIA alone and not some of the other monolines as well?

We ultimately shorted MBIA, FSA, Ambac, and others. Our approach requires deep, fundamental research, and it takes an enormous amount of time to research any one of these companies. Our timing was terrible on MBIA, but it eventually paid off. By contrast, our timing was very good on the other mortgage and bond insurers such as Radian, PMI, Ambac, and FSA. Experience is learning from mistakes.

Q: Have you seen that regulators are now more open to looking at criticisms from short sellers in the last few years?

Regulators do not have an easy job, especially with limited resources, and they have to focus on their priorities. I was a little disappointed with how long it took the regulators to see some of the issues that we had identified with MBIA. I think they have been much more responsive in the case of Herbalife. It did seem like a century between the time we shorted MBIA and when the SEC launched a formal investigation of the company. Their time-frames on these cases are not as aggressive as the private sector because they have to be careful. That is OK. I have a lot of respect for the SEC and FTC. I think they will ultimately get to the right answer on Herbalife.

I think the SEC has a lot of respect for the short sellers. As long as you disclose your interests (i.e., that you are shorting the stock), they have no issues in taking information from short sellers. They will use it to point them in the right direction in their investigations.

Q: When do you prefer to make a short bet using derivatives over cash equity?

The problem with short selling is that the upside is limited and the downside is unlimited. Derivatives are a good way to mitigate that risk. I would rather buy CDS than short a stock. You risk much less capital and you can make much more money.

Q: Is your investment horizon shorter with long-term puts than the CDS?

We can extend them so they are not necessarily shorter term. Of course, there is a cost to extend options.

Q: Can you describe the series of events in your research process that changed your investment outlook on Fannie Mae and Freddie Mac from bear to bull?

The stock prices declined and basically went to zero. [*chuckles*] They have a dominant market position and they offer a valuable service. The world has changed meaningfully in last six years since the depths of financial crisis. Housing markets have recovered. Interest rates are still very low. Their losses have declined. In fact, they over-reserved by $140 billion, and these reserves are in the process of being reversed. There are a number of proposals to wind down Freddie and Fannie. They were government agencies whose profits were taken away in an illegal action. There was no one single event that changed our minds. We became bullish after the facts changed.

Q: Is it easier to get the attention of Congress and regulators as a bull to your potential solutions on bringing Fannie and Freddie out of conservatorship?

We have made no effort to get their attention or to lobby them. We floated some thoughts in a 110-page presentation at the Ira Sohn Conference. It has made its way to the Congress and people are looking at it. The best solution to the problem will hopefully drive a favorable outcome for shareholders.

Q: How significant are macroeconomic indicators and cycles in your investment decisions?

We try to minimize macro risks in selecting the companies we invest in. As a result, we don't need to pay as much attention to macro factors in determining the likely outcome for the companies we own.

Q: Could you talk about some value traps that you decided to pass as an investment idea?

We have seen value traps that result from the inability to influence management as a result of a control shareholder who behaves economically irrationally.

Q: Do you look think troubled industries can be value traps (something like coal)?

The coal industry is likely in long-term secular decline because of its environmental impact. We generally try to avoid businesses that are similarly disadvantaged.

Q: What advice would have for a recent graduate or an aspiring professional investor?

I would say you should find a job at a firm whose investment philosophy and principles you respect. You should try to work with people you can trust and admire and learn from your and their mistakes. Good will come from that.

Recap

- Bill Ackman has adopted Graham and Buffett's approach about margin of safety—that is, a wide spread between the price you pay and value. Beyond that, the key element for him is very high quality of the business.

- When passive investors think the status quo will not change, an active investor can buy the company where he or she can change things and have a competitive advantage.
- Margin and leverage are dangerous sources of capital because you can be wiped out when the market crashes.
- The problem with short selling is that the upside is limited and downside is unlimited. Derivatives are good way to mitigate that risk.

8

Papa Bear

Coattailing Marquee Investors or Betting Against Them?

Be neither a conformist nor a rebel, for they are really the same
thing. Find your own path, and stay on it.
—PAUL VIXIE

YOU JUST HEARD A FAMOUS investor announce a short position
at a conference or on television. Congratulations, you found a
short thesis along with a catalyst—but so did the rest of the market. The stock takes a quick dive and easy profits are probably off
the table. You may not even be able to short the stock at this point
if it falls more than 10 percent, which would prompt the exchange
to impose a short sale restriction on the stock. If you are able to
short the stock at this point, you face the risk that the stock snaps
back. The famous investor is probably exiting at this point, and
new bulls are probably stepping in.

Typically, well-publicized shorts become crowded trades; it is
extremely hard to make long-term bearish bets on such stocks,
even if you agree with the bear. Increased borrowing costs, short
sale restrictions, and stock volatility are some of the key impediments to coattailing short trades. Such shorts can get even more
complicated with public outrage from regulators, promoters, and
other bulls.

If you want to coattail the marquee investor, it may be a wise idea to do your own research in addition to understanding his or her short thesis. If you find yourself on the other side of this trade after your initial research, you also want to double-check your facts because you are up against a smart investor with great financial resources and research ability. Your ray of hope in a contrarian bet is that the smart investor is human and may not be right 100 percent of the time.

This chapter presents a few well-publicized short stories to provide great insight into the research presented by reputed short sellers. I begin with the example of Herbalife, a highly controversial stock, where coattailing the bear would have been rough. Next, I argue how it made sense to bet against the long case for Banco Popular. I also cite an example of a short that did not work for the bear and an example where it made sense to bet with the bears. The chapter concludes with a brief discussion of analyst downgrades.

CASE STUDY: HERBALIFE (HLF)

Act I: Bear attack on Herbalife

Herbalife is a multilevel marketing company that sells weight management and nutrition products. Herbalife became public at the end of 2004 at $14 per share and hit an all-time high of $50 in 2008, but the Lehman Brothers crisis pushed the stock back to its initial public offering price levels. However, Herbalife stock had enjoyed a great streak since 2009, rising 4.5× to hit a new all-time high of $72.23 on April 26, 2012. During this second act of the stock, the revenues (excluding shipping and handling charges) increased from $2.3 billion to $3.4 billion, and the gross profit increased from $1.8 billion to ~$2.8 billion.

Five days later, on May 1, 2012, David Einhorn of Greenlight Capital appeared on Herbalife's earnings call to quiz management on its hierarchy of distributors and why the company stopped breaking out figures categorizing its lower-end distributors as self-consumers, small retailers, or potential sales leaders. "We can easily provide the exact same breakout going forward if you would like that sent to you and our investors," replied John DeSimone, Herbalife's chief financial officer (CFO). "Our objective is to be completely transparent."[1]

A full decade earlier, Einhorn had announced his short position on Allied Capital at the Ira Sohn Conference. After a long battle with Allied Capital and an ensuing investigation by the SEC, Einhorn was proved right. He already had a successful record short selling financial firms—a streak he continued with his successful short on Lehman Brothers in 2008. It is no wonder that the market's reaction to Einhorn's questioning on Herbalife was imminent; the company's shares fell three days in a row by 20 percent, 6 percent, and 12 percent, from $70.32 to $46.20.

However, Einhorn had not yet announced any short position on Herbalife; it was widely speculated that he would disclose his short position at the upcoming Ira Sohn Conference. However, he did not even mention Herbalife at the conference on May 16, 2012, ending the speculation on Herbalife to be his short idea. The stock rose 17 percent that day to $49.51, but then fell 10 percent the next day. Over the next three months, Herbalife stock crept back to over $50, as the company beat street estimates and raised guidance in its July 31 earnings release.

In its September 18, 2012, article, "You Have Been Einhorned," the *Wall Street Journal* suggested that Einhorn's bearish calls moved markets more significantly than his bullish ones. While Einhorn had still not publicly announced a short position in Herbalife, the stock began sliding for four days, down 10 percent from $52.53 on September 14 to $47.10 on September 20.

Act II: New bear attacks Herbalife

The Ira Sohn Conference on December 19, 2012, was a different story. Bill Ackman made a 334-page presentation, "Who Wants to be a Millionaire," making a detailed bear case for Herbalife. Ackman's thesis alleged that Herbalife was a pyramid scheme, where money at the top was made from losses suffered by people at the bottom of the pyramid.

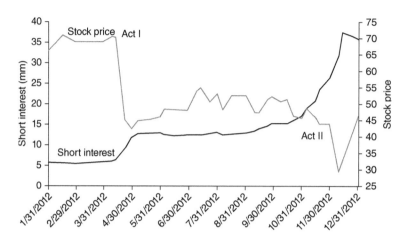

FIGURE 8.1 HLF short interest and stock prices. *Source:* Bloomberg.

Bill Ackman is a reputed activist investor who questioned the AAA rating of MBIA in 2002 (see chapter 7). His firm wagered a short bet on MBIA stock, bought credit default swaps on MBIA bonds, and stuck to their guns on the MBIA short for six years. During this time, his firm was also investigated by the New York Attorney General and the Securities and Exchange Commission (SEC); however, his thesis eventually was proven right in December 2007, when MBIA disclosed $8.1 billion of collateralized debt obligation exposure backed by risky home loan securities.[2] His short bet on MBIA made millions in profits.

Ackman's bear thesis on Herbalife argued that pyramid schemes are inherently fraudulent and must eventually collapse. His firm hosted a website to support his thesis (http://factsaboutherbalife .com). Herbalife stock went into a tailspin as Ackman doubted the legitimacy of their business model. The stock fell 12 percent on his announcement and continued to fall three days in a row by 9.75 percent, 19.08 percent, and 4.44 percent, from $42.50 to $26.06.

Act III: Bulls plow in, tug-of-war ensues, shorts squeezed

Herbalife stock rose 12 percent on December 31, 2012, and continued to rise another 10 percent as Herbalife's chief executive officer (CEO) defiantly presented his case during an analyst meeting on January 3, 2013. Shorts had little idea what brewed behind the stock rebound. A week later, Dan Loeb of Third Point announced an 8.24 percent stake in Herbalife; soon after, traders speculated that Carl Icahn had taken a large stake in Herbalife. The stock found life support with potential involvement of two reputed activist investors, rising another 15 percent.

On January 24, 2013, the *Wall Street Journal* reported that Einhorn had covered his short position on Herbalife for a profit, but the stock did not react much to the report. On the same day, Carl Icahn said in an interview with Bloomberg that he did not respect Ackman and did not like how Ackman had publicly attacked Herbalife; however, he did not disclose a stake in Herbalife. Icahn and Ackman both called in to a CNBC show during the next trading day to lash out at each other. The stock ended up by 5.7 percent that day.

In another twist, rumors of an Federal Trade Commission (FTC) conference call on pyramid schemes surfaced the following week, sending Herbalife stock down 10 percent. Herbalife continued to fall another 10 percent for the next week until the *New York Post* reported on February 4, 2013, that the FTC was investigating claims of pyramid schemes. The stock dropped 13 percent in premarket trading on the news, but recovered losses as Herbalife said it was not a subject of FTC investigation and demanded a correction from the *New York Post*.

A tug of war between bulls and bears ensued as Carl Ichan disclosed a 12.8 percent stake in Herbalife on February 14, sending the stock up 22 percent in after-market trading. CNBC reported on July 31, 2013, that Soros Funds Management took a large stake in Herbalife. Bill Ackman filed a complaint with the SEC against Soros Funds, alleging that it broke insider trading laws. Herbalife stock nearly doubled by August 18, 2013. However, I believed that the jury was still out on Herbalife stock as Ackman is known to have bounced back in the past by holding on to his position.

Act IV: Ackman replaces short position with puts, federal investigations are opened

Bill Ackman cut his short stock position by more than 40 percent around September 2013 and replaced it with long-term, over-the-counter put options while vowing to take his Herbalife bet "to the end of the world." On March 12, 2014, Herbalife announced that FTC had opened an investigation into its operations. Herbalife was down 10 percent on the news. A month later, *Financial Times* reported that the U.S. Department of Justice and the FBI had opened a criminal probe into Herbalife. The stock fell 15 percent on the news to the low 50s and traded down to the low 40s at the time of publication of this book.

Takeaway
The Herbalife story shows many things that can go wrong in coattailing smart investors. Shorts with the public involvement of activist investors become a hotbed for traders and often result in violent movements in the stock price. Tactical short-term trading in such stocks may bring swift profits, but regular trading in such stocks can also be a recipe for disaster.

Smart Investors Are Human: Contrarian Bets

While only a handful of investors publicly announce their short positions, a much larger number of long investors often publicly advocate their long positions. Every once in a while, long investors tend to underestimate or overlook the risks to their thesis, begging a closer scrutiny of the risks. Banco Popular (BPOP) seemed to be such a case in April 2010, when some hedge funds held a large position and mentioned the stock favorably at an investor conference. After a quick glance at the loan quality of BPOP, I became curious to look more closely at BPOP's public filings.

CASE STUDY:
BANCO POPULAR (BPOP)

BPOP was trading at 1.1x book value while its asset quality (table 8.1) continued to deteriorate. A few things stood out as I looked further into the company's assets: 70 percent of BPOP's assets were in Puerto Rico, where the local governments were under great budget constraints. Level III assets, or thinly traded assets with no observable market, constituted a relatively high proportion (~4 percent) of BPOP's assets. During the financial crisis, banks had come under severe pressure for overestimating the value of their Level III assets.[3]

Table 8.1

Valuation/asset quality		Consensus	
Price to earnings (P/E) LTM	NM	Rev 10	$1,785.46
Price to tangible book value (P/Tang B) LTM	1.1x	Revinttype 11	$1,853.30
Price/book (P/B)	0.8x	EPS 10	($0.54)
Price/sales (P/S) LTM	3.4x	P/E 10	−5.8x
Non-performing loans (NPL)/loans	9.6x	EPS 11	$0.27
NPL/assets	6.6x	P/E 11	11.6x
Non-performing assets (NPA)/equity	94.60%	Buy/ H/ Sell	2/4/2
Allowance/charge off	122.80%	S&P rating	B-/downgrade
Earnings before interest and taxes (EBIT)/int LTM	NA	S&P outlook	Negative

Source: BPOP SEC filings.

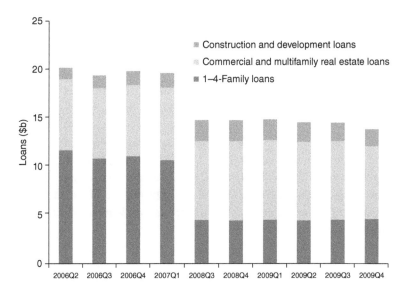

FIGURE 8.2 BPOP loan composition. *Source:* BPOP SEC filings.

BPOP did not seem to be provisioning adequately for potential losses from Level III assets and nonperforming assets (NPAs), raising questions about the quality of their earnings (table 8.2). BPOP's stock price, however, seemed to indicate that NPAs had peaked, in stark contrast with the BPOP CFO's statement in a Sterne Agee conference in February: "There is no way that the company can make money with this level of provision for loan losses (6 percent), we were caught with very large portfolios of real estate market through HELOC loans, construction loans, mortgage loans that now we're paying the price for it."

The BPOP CFO raised red flags when he mentioned that he was flabbergasted as to why his accountants were asking for higher levels of reserves when BPOP knew its borrowers well. There seemed to be many reasons mentioned during the conference that justified the demand of the accountants to raise the reserve levels:

Table 8.2
BPOP snapshot of financials and key metrics

Stock data		Income statement (LTM)		Returns/capital structure	
Stock price	$3.12	Rev (mm) LTM	$591.95	ROA LTM	-1.50%
Market cap (millions)	$2,002	Op Inc (mm) LTM	($543.63)	ROE LTM	-19.08%
Shares out (float %)	640 million (98%)	Dil. EPS ($/sh) LTM	$0.24	TARP received	$935 mm
Enterprise value (millions)	NA	Net interest margin	3.50%	TARP warrants at $7 strike	20.9 mm
52-Week range	1.0–3.7	Efficiency ratio	NM	ROC LTM	0.00%
Average volume	1.82	EPS (% 1 year)	NM	Tier 1 ratio	9.81%
Average volume (% of Sh.)	0.28%	Rev (% 1 year)	-47.00%	Core tier 1 ratio	6.39%
Short int (% of Sh. out)	1.70%	EPS (% 2 year)	-3506.70%	Total capital ratio	11.13%
Insider	1.40%	Rev (% 2 year CAGR)	-43.30%	Leverage ratio	7.5×

Source: BPOP SEC filings.

Puerto Rico had an overhang of large inventory of unsold housing, even though prices had not collapsed like the mainland U.S. market. Everyone was losing money in Puerto Rico, with the exception of probably one small investment bank.

At the time, 20,000 construction units remained unsold—a relatively high number—pushing the nonperforming loan level of the construction portfolio to a staggering 45 percent. The loan-to-value ratio on mortgages had risen to 100 percent from 80 percent at the time of origination. In addition to these core problems, BPOP stock had an overhang of $900 million in TARP equity and 29 million TARP warrants. While BPOP had reduced its reliance on wholesale funding in the last two years through a stronger deposit base and stood to benefit from a consolidation of banks in Puerto Rico, the stock seemed to be a value trap.

With NPA/equity at 94.6 percent, there was a very high likelihood that equity could be wiped out in the event of a worsening economy in Puerto Rico. Because banks are highly regulated entities and required to maintain threshold capital levels (Tier 1 capital, etc.), it was highly likely that BPOP would need to raise additional equity to strengthen its balance sheet.

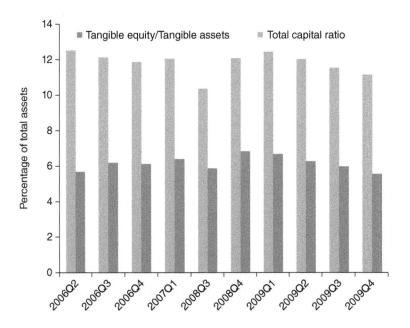

FIGURE 8.3 BPOP capital ratios. *Source:* BPOP SEC filings.

How Did It Play Out?

BPOP shares traded below $3 per share for the rest of 2010 and briefly traded up to $3.5 per share in the first quarter of 2011. They reported a quarterly profit on July 20, 2011; however, the stock was down for the year at $2.56 per share. A week later, BPOP stock fell below $2 per share as S&P downgraded the U.S. ratings on August 5, 2011. The stock continued to slide, hitting a low of $1.12 per share on December 19, 2011.

Takeaway

Banks have significant financial leverage, which accentuates the impact of poor-quality assets. They are highly regulated entities and required to maintain threshold capital levels (Tier 1 capital, etc.). High NPA ratios can often force banks to raise equity to strengthen their balance sheet.

CASE STUDY:
AMAZON.COM (AMZN)

David Einhorn was critical of Amazon's profitability at the Ira Sohn Conference on May 16, 2012. He said that Amazon had not grown its profits in tandem with sales and Amazon's future is a riddle.[4] Unlike most of Einhorn's shorts, Amazon stock rose 25 percent over the next year after his announcement. Amazon may have seemed to trade at a high valuation; however, it was hard to question the pace and drivers of their sales growth—the factors that could sustain Amazon's stock price momentum.

I had looked at Amazon as a potential short in 2010 and decided to pass because I could not find any clear issues with their business model. While Amazon did not have a retail footprint, their growth trajectory seemed strikingly similar to Walmart's during their growth years. If Amazon could continue growth at a pace similar to Walmart's, a short case for Amazon did not stand a chance.

Amazon's net sales in 2009 stood at ~$25 billion, with a net income of ~$900 million. Walmart's net sales in 1990 were ~$25 billion, with a net income of ~$1 billion. Walmart multiplied its sales by 16 times over the next twenty years at 15 percent compound annual growth rate (CAGR) to $400 billion and grew its net income 14 times to ~$14 billion. During this period, Walmart increased the number of superstores from less than 100 to 2,747, and the groceries category as a percent of Walmart's sales increased from 18 percent to 51 percent. With $400 billion in sales, Walmart traded at 13–14 times its earnings.

While Amazon's sales had grown at ~24.4 percent CAGR since 2000, the law of large numbers could slow down the rate of growth, as their sales had grown from a much smaller base of

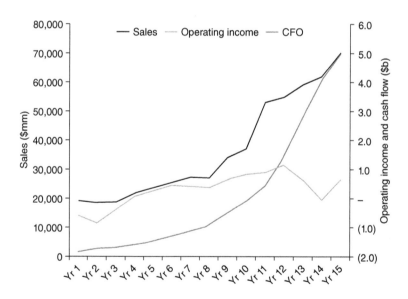

FIGURE 8.4 Amazon sales growth from ~$2 billion to over $75 billion 1998–2013. *Source:* Amazon SEC filings.

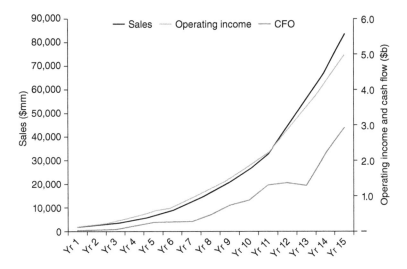

FIGURE 8.5 Walmart sales growth from ~$2 billion to over $75 billion 1980–1995. *Source:* Walmart SEC filings.

$2.8 billion in 2000 to $24.5 billion in 2009. If Amazon's growth slowed down to 15 percent, it would take them twenty years to reach the size of Walmart. At 15 percent CAGR growth, Amazon's sales would reach $100 billion in ten years and net income would reach $4 billion. If Amazon continued to fetch a growth multiple of 20 times the price-to-earnings ratio, their market cap would be $80 billion. Amazon's market cap in 2011 was $80 billion.

It was easy to make an argument that Amazon was not a cheap stock. However, Amazon silenced its critics as it leapfrogged expectations by growing sales at 36.5 percent CAGR from $24.5 billion in 2009 to $61 billion in 2012, mainly through international growth. While Amazon generated little profits in 2012, as Einhorn pointed out, Amazon did not seem to face growth issues in the near future from competition or other factors.

In his 2012 letter to shareholders, Jeff Bezos, Amazon founder and CEO, noted the complaints on profitability: "Our heavy investments in Prime, AWS, Kindle, digital media, and customer experience in general strike some as too generous, shareholder indifferent, or even at odds with being a for-profit company." He went on to argue that doling out just-in-time improvements is too risky in the modern fast-moving world and taking a long-term customer-centric view would ultimately align the interests of customers and shareholders.[5]

Bezos had been advocating this focus on the long term since 1997 and successfully delivered on his promise. Capital expenditures at Amazon continued at the rate of $2.5 billion to $3.5 billion per year at the expense of profitability, in line with Bezos's mantra for success in the long term. Clearly, pointing to poor profitability and high valuations was not reason enough to short Amazon—even for smart investors—as the history of proven growth at Amazon outweighed profit concerns. A short case would need to clearly articulate why Amazon could face slower growth and identify near-term threats.

Takeaway

High valuation and poor margins are not always good enough reasons to short a fast-growing company. A CEO with a proven track record would attract loyal investors who are willing to overlook short-term issues and obfuscate short sellers.

CASE STUDY:
APOLLO GROUP (APOL)

Jim Chanos was an early short on the for-profit education sector at the Ira Sohn Conference in 2009. He argued that these companies derived 80–90 percent of their revenues from student loans backed by federal taxpayers—a business model that abused taxpayers' dollars. A year later, Steve Eisman of Frontpoint Partners presented his short case on the same sector at the Ira Sohn Conference, arguing that for-profits claimed ~25 percent of the

$89 billion of Federal Title IV loans, and these claims required greater scrutiny.

Apollo stock had fallen from the $60 per share range in 2010 to $46 per share in July 2011, after Apollo withdrew guidance citing declining enrollments and increased regulatory pressure on the for-profit industry. Apollo group shares yielded free cash yield of over 10 percent based on historical cash flow, and one of my clients asked me to take a look at it.[6]

While researching Apollo Group, the owner of University of Phoenix, I focused on their free cash flow, specifically to determine if the free cash flow seemed sustainable in the face of declining enrollments. This would be central to a bull thesis because it would allow Apollo to aggressively buy back its shares and boost its earnings per share.

An earnings sensitivity analysis showed that the stock was already pricing in a 15–20 percent decline in enrollments over the next two years. However, the stock was not pricing the risk to Apollo's business model from the regulatory risks pointed out by shorts. High reliance on Title IV loans remained a major concern. According to Apollo's filings, "University of Phoenix generated 88

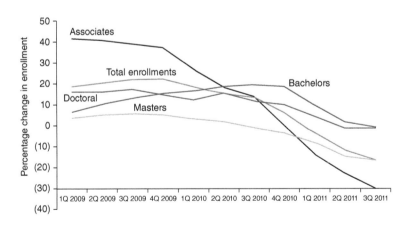

FIGURE 8.6 University of Phoenix enrollment trend, year over year percent change. *Source:* Apollo SEC filings.

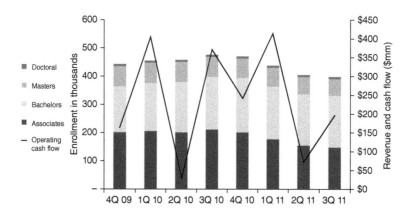

FIGURE 8.7 Apollo Group enrollment mix and operating cash flow. *Source:* Apollo SEC filings.

percent of its cash basis revenue for eligible tuition and fees during fiscal year 2010 and 86 percent in 2009 from the receipt of Title IV financial aid program funds under the 90/10 rule."

Under the 90/10 rule, Apollo Group could become ineligible to participate in Title IV programs for at least two fiscal years if, for any two consecutive fiscal years, it derived more than 90 percent of its cash basis revenue from Title IV loans. Apollo stated that it was likely to exceed 90 percent in fiscal year 2012 due to the expiration of the loan limit increases relief in July 2011. If Apollo continued to exceed the 90 percent threshold in 2013, its business model faced serious questions. I agreed with the bears and recommended against buying Apollo.

Analyst Downgrades

Wall Street analysts cover a number of stocks and routinely upgrade or downgrade their stocks. These rating changes may not always be prognostic; for example, an analyst may choose to downgrade a stock after it falls 20 percent on missing earnings numbers. In such a case, the stock mostly prices the downgrade risk. However, if such downgrades result from a prognosis of fundamental issues related to accounting, competition, channel stuffing, capacity, executive turnover, etc., the stock merits a closer look at the issues. Such analyst downgrades may lead to good short ideas. I will cover some short ideas from a successful short-focused research firm in the next chapter.

Recap

- Well-publicized shorts become crowded trades. It is extremely hard to make long-term bearish bets on such stocks, even if you agree with the bear.
- Increased borrowing costs, short sale restrictions, and stock volatility are some of the key impediments to coat-tailing short trades.
- Long investors can underestimate and overlook risks with the investment. Close examination of these risks can generate short ideas.
- High valuation and poor margins are not always good enough reasons to short a fast-growing company.
- Analyst downgrades from prognosis of fundamental issues related to accounting, competition, channel stuffing, capacity, executive turnover, etc., may lead to good short ideas.

9

Off Wall Street

Two Decades of Successful Shorting

> The main thing short ideas have in common is that their business
> model is not going to produce the sales and earnings that are
> expected by the market.
> —MARK ROBERTS

An Interview with Mark Roberts

Mark Roberts left Fidelity to start Off Wall Street in 1990 to
serve a small but growing hedge fund industry. Roberts found
hedge funds to be the most dynamic (yet underserved) part of the
investing business and saw a clear opportunity to write research
for hedge funds. On May 1, 1990, he published his first piece
titled "TCBY Is in Deep Yogurt," and successfully sold it to hedge
funds for $5,000 per copy. Since 1993, Off Wall Street has closed
out 433 positions, with 343 winners and 90 losers—an impressive
batting average of more than 80 percent.

His notable recommendations include the Enron sell report,
which received praise at the Senate Enron hearings, particularly
from Senators Joseph Lieberman and Barbara Boxer. During the
Senate hearing, "The Watchdogs Didn't Bark: Enron and the
Wall Street Analysts," Senator Lieberman praised Roberts's variant view on Enron. He noted that Mark Roberts, unlike Wall

Street analysts, had diagnosed key problems with Enron: shrinking profit margins, related party transactions, and poor cash flow and returns from recurring operations.[1]

I first met Mark Roberts in 2008 at his Cambridge office and was inspired to start my own research firm. I have remained in touch with him and discuss my own short ideas with him from time to time. When I reached out to him for an exclusive interview for my book, he generously agreed to share some of his past research work as well.

Off Wall Street's short ideas have been based on a variety of reasons, such as accounting issues, business model issues, and competitive threats. I believe that the readers will greatly benefit from Roberts's insight on researching short ideas and related short stories. I have included his past short ideas in this chapter, along with the following interview.

Q: How did you decide to start Off Wall Street?

I have an undergraduate and graduate degrees in French literature and art history. I joined my brother in a family business in the early 1970s to run the largest steel distribution company in New England. During the Carter years, we sold our steel businesses when the interest rates were very high. I separated with my brother to get involved in technology business and started the largest franchise chain of retail software stores. Retail software business was a passing phenomenon, and I sold out my interest in the business in 1984. I moved to New York, where I became interested in investing. I thought, wouldn't it be nice if I could make money in the stock market and not have to go back to "real work"? But I was thoroughly unprepared for such a career. I began to look for a job where I could learn how to analyze stocks.

I met Mark Boyar at Boyar Asset Management, who was kind to offer me a job to write research in his publication "Asset Analysis

Focus." Mark did [me] a big favor because I was totally unqualified, except I was a good writer and had practical business experience. After a year, I moved back to Boston to write research for a brokerage house whose main client was Fidelity, and I eventually landed at Fidelity. During my one and a half years at Fidelity, I realized that hedge funds were the most interesting and dynamic side of the investing business. There was not much research for hedge funds because most research was long and nothing short, for which they had a clear mandate. I left Fidelity to write short ideas and peddle them to hedge funds.

Q: How did you come across your first short idea? How difficult was it to sell your first idea?

While I was putting together my business plan, I worked as a consultant for Seth Klarman at Baupost, where I learned a lot about value investing. At Baupost, an investor approached me because of my background in franchising. He asked me if I knew about TCBY enterprises. I started looking into the TCBY franchising chain and realized it was a can of worms. That became my first short idea and I published my first piece on May 1, 1990. At first, I used to give clever names to my research pieces and even put cartoons to make them look like *The New Yorker*, something like James Grant does today. My research was titled "TCBY Is in Deep Yogurt," and I successfully sold it for $5,000 a copy to a few hedge funds.

However, I quickly realized that business model won't work because it was too much effort to sell the research. I wanted someone to put me on retainer. Meanwhile, I was working on a second idea, Summit Technology, a photorefractive keratectomy laser company, which eventually went bankrupt after a long battle with me. While I was working on Summit, I managed to get a hedge fund to put me on retainer. My next idea was CompUSA. These ideas were well received and I picked up another retainer and I was in business.

Q: What drove Summit Technology to bankruptcy?

Summit Technology was overly promotional with an inferior laser. They tried to expand to other businesses, like laser centers, and they overreached. David Muller, who ran the business, drove Summit into bankruptcy by being aggressively promotional.

Q: How has your research style evolved over the last 23.5 years?

I actually think that nothing much has changed over these years. We are not doing anything too much differently, but probably doing it better with more experience and more staff. The only change through all the ups and downs is that we have become more risk averse. We have learned to avoid problems by avoiding certain kinds of potentially short stories. We have been burned by certain types of short ideas and we have lowered our risk profile.

Q: What are some of the reasons you would not short a stock?

Generally speaking, the dangerous short stories involve a long runway of sales growth. Investors can pay up for multiple years of sales growth in advance. Some of these companies can keep growing for a good period of time as well. We tend to avoid companies with good growth track records and a long runway of growth.

Q: How do you determine the runway of growth for such companies?

We look at the potential market size and try to determine if the market does exist. If the company has a good growth track record and is well managed, it may also fetch high valuation; however, the high valuation does not matter.

Q: What do you see differently about short ideas and long ideas?

When we look at long ideas, we look at risk first. We try to limit downside on the long ideas and our first goal is not to lose money. Secondly, we look for stocks that are not well liked, where investor sentiment has changed due to missed earnings, where investors do not like the management or something else has changed. We are value investors on the long side.

On the short side, it is quite different. Clearly, shorting is an inherently risky business because the math works against you. As you know, you can lose multiples of your investment, but you cannot make more than 100 percent on your investment. On the short side, we are interested in limiting risk, but shorting stocks is inherently risky. We look for short ideas with high valuation where we feel we cannot get too blown away and we think that the valuation is arguably 30–40 percent too high, provided our thesis about the future of the business will play out the way we want.

There is no formula to find the short ideas. The main characteristic they all have in common is that their business model is not going to produce the sales and earnings that are expected by the market. There will be a psychological disappointment, which will change the way investors view the company and create the revaluation downwards.

Q: Do you think it is harder to generate alpha on shorts than longs? Do you see greater interest in short ideas from your clients?

Our business is mainly to come up with short ideas for clients. Short sellers are not as highly rewarded as their long counterparts, while it is much more challenging to make money shorting. There is a tendency among hedge funds not to be short sellers; however, they have a charter to sell short. Most hedge funds think that they are better on the long side and they can make more money in longs. They concentrate on longs and hedge because they are trying to protect capital in a down market, but not too many funds short sell as their primary strategy.

Q: How important are channel checks and surveys, etc.?

If you are a short seller, by the nature of what you are trying to do, you are seeking the type of information that is not widely distributed and is not consensus thinking. Short ideas naturally need more discovery to reach conviction than longs because the information is harder to come by. It takes a lot more work and interviewing to find sources of information not available in the mainstream.

That said, we do not channel check. The most common example is calling stores to ask how they are selling during a time frame. We are not short-term oriented and we are looking for an investment thesis, so we do not find channel checking useful in the traditional sense.

Q: Do you think it is more important to identify short-term catalysts for shorts than longs?

We do not try to find short-term catalysts. We try to find medium-term investments where we expect the business model to not produce the sales and earnings that are expected. The catalyst is always a change in the investor psychology, which can be triggered by a number of factors such as sales miss, earning miss, accounting problems, competitive change.

Q: What is your process to find the short ideas?

There is no easy way to find shorts. It is like writing short stories. You always wonder where the next idea will come from or if there are any ideas around at all. Short ideas can come from screens, reading, talking to other investors, and we do all of the above. If it were so simple, everyone would do it successfully. That does not happen. We use all avenues to find ideas.

Q: Can you talk about one of your early ideas? Maybe Enron?

Enron was a great story. We were the only firm to publish a sell recommendation, and our research on Enron was quite extraordinary. Lots of people talked about their accounting, insider transactions, problems with the CFO [chief financial officer], but we demonstrated why Enron's business model did not work. When you see accounting issues, it is generally because there are problems with the business and managers resort to earnings manipulation to cover up the issues. We never think of accounting issues as a reason to sell the stock per se. They are symptoms of larger problems and our job as analysts is to understand those problems. Accounting issues in themselves can be solved by good management if they have a good business model. But they cannot overcome fundamental business problems.

Q: Have you found it helpful to focus on any specific areas in the financial statements to spot accounting issues?

Not really. When there is a large difference between a company's generally accepted accounting principles earnings and what the company claims as adjusted earnings—management of companies in any industry can use such techniques and the more promotional companies, with an agenda to advance their stock price, have an incentive to use more aggressive reporting techniques.

Q: Could you talk about an example where the stock did not perform as expected?

Back in the day, we were shorting AOL mainly on the accounting issues related to amortization of customer acquisition expense, specifically the length of time that they were amortizing. We got the issue right and the company was forced by the SEC [Securities and Exchange Commision] to eventually restate the accounting. However, we got the fundamentals of the business wrong, at least at that time. We hugely underestimated the size of the market, which was so much bigger with a long runway. This is the type of lesson that I was talking about. You can get the pieces right but the big picture wrong.

Q: So, when do you decide to hold or fold in such a case?

That is a tough one because we are not portfolio managers. We do fundamental research and our timing can be off. We do not like to close position where we get the fundamentals right just because the stock has gone against us. On the other hand, we have certainly witnessed some error if things go too far. We may have understood the company but not the investor sentiment. That is not a fundamental research error but an error in judging investor behavior.

We close positions when we think that a change in the nature of business alters our thesis or when our thesis is just not playing out or when there is no evidence that we are right. Sometimes our thesis will play out but it can take too long. We closed our position out of exhaustion in such a case. Overall, we try to produce investment quality ideas and not trading ideas.

Q: You recommend a short idea and it goes down 30 percent. You close the recommendation and it comes back up to where you recommended. Do you recommend them again?

Many times. For example, we successfully shorted F5 Networks (FFIV) on three occasions, twice recently. You can get a turnover in the investor base and new investors have not learned from the old investors. Old investors got discouraged by a story that now a whole new group of investors believes in.

Q: What changed about F5 Networks each time?

First time, the company missed numbers and the stock went down. We closed the position. New investors did not believe that the miss was related to fundamental reasons and the stock ran back up again. From our standpoint, the short thesis remained intact.

Q: How significant are macroeconomic indicators and cycles in your short analysis?

We only look at macro information in order to help us see the areas with overvalued names. We do not make macro predictions. It is not what we do and we do what we are good at.

Q: Have you recommended shorting commodities-linked stocks in the past?

We have not done too much in the commodities space. We have done more on the long side. We do not make a short call on economically sensitive stock because it is a call on the economic cycle and not a fundamental business call. It is not what we do.

Q: Have you recommended any value traps—stocks that seem cheap but have more potential downside?

We tend to be more long on the value traps. Sometimes, we recommend a stock that will go up but it does not. I call them value traps. Value traps are not good short candidates from our standpoint because the risk rewards are not favorable. Good management can do a lot for the company that has good revenue stream. It is hard to handicap.

Q: Have you looked at recent initial public offerings that trade at 10–20× sales, especially companies that made follow-on offerings?

No. We are not interested in such companies because their markets and business models are too open-ended and they are very hard to gauge.

Q: Do you stay away from stocks that engage high-profile investors or stocks with high short interest?

Yes. We only get involved where we can add value and do some differentiated research. We want to be original.

Off Wall Street Short Stories

Off Wall Street has contributed some of their past short recommendations for this book. I have tried my best to preserve the core analysis while presenting them in an abridged version in relevant parts of my framework throughout the book. The following case of Liquidity Services demonstrates where the threat of loss of key client contracts could impair a business model.

CASE STUDY:
LIQUIDITY SERVICES INC. (LQDT)

LQDT, based in Washington, DC, operates leading online auction marketplaces for surplus and salvage assets. It sells merchandise under consignment and profit-sharing arrangements, as well as for its own account. LQDT was predominantly a federal government contractor several years ago, with U.S. Department of Defense (DoD) contracts accounting for 77 percent of gross merchandise value (GMV), or total sales proceeds for all items it sold in 2005. Since then, their commercial GMV had grown faster to become a much larger portion of the business, with one-third of the commercial GMV growth coming from acquisitions.

Off Wall Street noticed that DoD accounted for ~24 percent of GMV and 74 percent of 2012 operating profits, much higher than investors realized with respect to operating profits. Its subsequent research showed that recent growth in DoD business appeared unsustainable and a material portion of DoD revenue was at risk from base realignments coming to an end and troops returning from Iraq and Afghanistan.

LQDT had two contracts with the DoD: a scrap and a surplus contract. There was less financial data available on surplus contracts than scrap contracts, under which LQDT retained 23–25 percent of net profits on scrap sales. More important, the surplus contract term would end in December 2013, and DoD could introduce a competitive bid process. (This information is based on Off Wall Street's discussion with sources familiar with the DoD process.)

LQDT also had significant customer concentration in its commercial business, with Walmart and Acer together accounting for ~50 percent of 2012 commercial GMV. A LQDT competitor told Off Wall Street that certain Walmart personnel in the reverse supply chain were furious after LQDT acquired Jacobs. They moved some uncontracted volumes away from Jacobs after learning that the contract was too favorable for LQDT, presumably at Walmart's expense. Jacobs derived 70 percent of its revenues from Walmart, and the loss of more contracts could significantly dent GMV growth.

Off Wall Street's report on July 1, 2012, caused the stock to plunge 25 percent, but it recovered most of its losses over the next two months. The recovery was short lived, as LQDT fell ~20 percent in October after reporting lower than expected September GMV data.

Source: Off Wall Street.

Recap

- **Avoid dangerous short stories that involve a long runway of sales growth. Investors can pay up for multiple years of sales growth. Look at the potential market size of growth companies to determine if the market exists. Avoid shorting companies with a good growth track record and management.**

- The main thing successful shorts have in common is that their business model is not going to produce the sales and earnings that are expected by the market. Psychological disappointment changes the way investors view the company and creates the revaluation downwards.
- Short ideas naturally need more discovery to reach conviction than longs because the information is harder to come by. It takes a lot more work and interviewing to find sources of information not available in the mainstream.
- Accounting issues are symptoms of larger problems. Accounting issues, in themselves, can be solved by good management if they have a good business model, but fundamental problems are hard to overcome.

PART III

Risks and Mechanics of Short Selling

10

When to Hold, When to Fold

Rule No. 1: Never lose money. Rule No. 2: Never forget rule No. 1.
—WARREN BUFFETT

THE 1980 GRAMMY-WINNING track by Kenny Rogers captures the essence of managing risk: "You got to know when to hold 'em, know when to fold 'em, know when to walk away, know when to run." Is it a surprise that many stock investors and traders love the games of poker and blackjack? Both poker and investing need at least three things to play: skills, philosophy, and money. Successful investors and poker players make insane bets only when odds are insanely in their favor. At the same time, they are not shy about cutting their losses or even folding early.

I have used various examples throughout the book to make the case that managing the risks associated with short positions is much harder than with long positions. Shorting a stock is like a hurdle race, where jumping over the short-term hurdles is as important as reaching the finish line—hurdles such as getting called on the stock, merger and acquisition (M&A) rumors, and short-sale restrictions.

How to Allocate Money Into Shorting Stocks

I watched my portfolio manager make allocation decisions during my early days on the buy side and later gained more secondhand knowledge from interacting with my clients, reading reports from a diverse set of portfolio managers, and watching the interviews of reputed investors. I returned to the buy side in 2014 to help manage U.S. stock portfolios at Columbia Threadneedle, which mostly employs a diversified strategy in managing investment portfolios, depending on the fund's investment mandate.

In the last year, I have managed two U.S. long-short portfolios with my partner and our capital allocation strategy has been evolved into a distinctly disciplined approach where we allocate capital into three distinct categories of stocks: core (cyclical and non-cyclical), growth compounders, and special situation stocks such that our top 15 to 20 stock allocations constitute half of the portfolio. On the other hand, the short portfolio tends to be diversified and we try to stay away from open-ended growth stories and acquisition risks.

In my interactions with various other mutual fund and hedge fund managers, I have largely found that their allocation strategy is an outcome of their investment charter and their own investing philosophy. Some managers strictly adhere to well-defined rules, such as limiting position sizes to 3 percent of the portfolio, while other managers make more concentrated ad-hoc bets.

There is also a wide range of views on risk management among professional money managers. Some managers formulaically review their investment thesis when the stock moves 20 percent against them and close out their position when the stock moves 30 percent against them. Some managers, such as Bill Ackman, can hold on to their high conviction idea for years, while others may even increase their bets when the stock moves materially against them.

Optimal allocation and prudent risk management can limit downside. Analyzing developments since the initial investment is critical to making allocation changes and risk management decisions. This chapter presents a few cases from an analyst's point of view on when it makes sense to hold or fold, as well as on the risks in shorting hot stocks or crowded shorts. I will share my experiences as a portfolio manager in the future editions of the book.

Hold When the Story Doesn't Change Materially

It is more an art than a science to analyze new developments that might alter your investment thesis. In some cases, a company's strategic decisions to fix large problems may seem as futile as fixing a broken leg with a Band-Aid. For example, Research in Motion promoted its new tablet product in 2011 in an attempt to distract investors from problems with its flagship Blackberry phones.

In other cases, Wall Street analysts can make short-term tactical buy recommendations on troubled companies. As we saw in the case of Office Depot, a bulge bracket analyst upgraded his recommendation from sell to neutral, citing his channel checks. The stock rose 10 percent on the upgrade. There was no evidence in his report to suggest that the company was working on a turnaround plan amid industry decline, and competitive issues remained. It made sense to hold our position and I remained bearish.

Troubled companies seem to attract more speculators and M&A rumors, as we saw in the case of telecom carriers. Companies can try to kick the can down the road by getting bigger through mergers, but they mostly fail to attract suitors on their terms. Their management can make unreasonably bullish forecasts, attracting new investors who underestimate the risks. The management keeps handholding Wall Street to unrealistic guidance and eventually disappoints everyone.

CASE STUDY:
F5 NETWORKS (FFIV)

F5 Networks designs and sells application delivery controllers (ADCs)—hardware appliances that allocate incoming traffic across servers in a data center. Bulls viewed F5, a major player in the load balancer market with over 50 percent market share and 30 percent operating margins, as a play on Internet traffic growth, data center virtualization, and cloud computing.

Off Wall Street formed a variant view when its research found that large data centers such as those operated by Amazon, Google, and Rackspace were bypassing F5's off-the-shelf ADC products to build their own custom equipment. The primary reason was cost. As more of the growth in computing power and data handling consolidated into such large entities in cloud computing, hardware vendors like F5 could benefit far less than what bulls expected.

F5 sold its hardware at very high prices (~$400,000 for the highest end appliance). Large-scale users could save half the price by building their own hardware from commodity components, and industry contacts confirmed that there were overwhelming incentives to do so. Resellers, who accounted for ~85 percent of F5 sales, were expecting enterprise hardware sales to decline and were shifting their business models away from hardware.

F5 faced increasing competition in hardware from A10 Networks, an emerging player that offered similar functionality at a lower price point. Software-only ADC vendors, such as Zeus (acquired by Riverbed), were gaining traction by offering similar functionality at a meaningfully lower price. A10 claimed to offer a $15,000 device that was comparable to a $60,000 F5 device. F5 struggled to compete as it sought to protect its hardware franchise.

After six quarters of decelerating growth, F5's product sales had accelerated in the March quarter of 2012. Wall Street expected this reacceleration to be sustained, while Off Wall Street believed that F5 would struggle to meet these expectations and the stock's valuation multiple would compress as challenges to F5's growth became more widely understood. F5 stock fell ~30 percent over the next six months from $130 to $90, as Off Wall Street had expected.

F5 Networks Repeat Short in 2013

F5 product sales continued to decelerate in 2012 and grew only 4 percent on a year-over-year basis in the December quarter. F5 management attributed the weakness to temporary macro weakness, and once again expected a recent hardware refresh to reaccelerate growth in product revenues to the high teens by the second half of 2013. Wall Street analysts expected F5's product revenue growth rates to be in the 20 percent range.

Off Wall Street remained skeptical, as its original short thesis on F5 had not changed materially. Its sources indicated that large-scale cloud providers and private clouds were moving toward a software-driven networking approach in which hardware is treated as a commoditized pool of assets. It issued a new short recommendation after the stock climbed back to $101 in February 2013. F5 stock fell ~30 percent again over the next six months, from $101 to ~$70, as it held onto its bearish position.

Source: Off Wall Street.

Fold When the Story Unfolds with Unexpected Material Developments

Market expectations begin to rise when troubled companies announce turnaround plans and investors buy into the plan. Investors can pay up for the stock in advance of the turnaround if they believe that the company has low leverage and it generates decent cash flow. Management can capitalize on investor enthusiasm by encouraging them to ignore short-term issues and focus on the longer-term turnaround goals. Investors may be inclined to remain hopeful, at least during the first year of a multiyear plan. It may make sense to fold if the stock rises by more than 30 percent, and then revisit the thesis when more clear evidence emerges.

CASE STUDY:
WESTERN UNION (WU)

Western Union fell ~30 percent to $12.73 after they reported third-quarter 2012 revenues that fell 3 percent short of consensus estimates. During the conference call, the Western Union chief executive officer (CEO) played down the competitive pricing atmosphere and blamed the miss on macroeconomic softness and tougher regulatory compliance norms. I began looking at the company when a client asked me if Western Union was a value stock.

Western Union spun off First Data in 2006 and derived 84 percent of its revenues from consumer money transfers through its 485,000 agents. Both send and receive agents were paid percentage commissions on revenue. The agent's primary business bore the costs of physical infrastructure and staff. Western Union had recently acquired Travelex's B2B business to boost its business payments solutions. It also tied up with MasterCard to enter the prepaid card business.[1]

My research indicated that the money transfer industry was highly fragmented. Western Union, the largest player with strong cash flows, faced competition from smaller new rivals such as Xoom,[2] and pricing pressure from incumbents such as MoneyGram (MGI) and Ria.[3] My analysis of Western Union's transaction economics (table 10.1) showed signs of structural decline in its unit pricing and profitability. While Western Union had authorized $550 million share buybacks and increased dividend payouts, it was aggressively cutting prices, which could continue the declining trend in profitability. Western Union seemed like a value trap.

I recommended against buying Western Union, but I did not want to recommend shorting it in light of buyback announcements after the stock's fall. I waited for the short recommendation until the stock rose ~15 percent leading up to the fourth-quarter earnings report in February 2013. The stock traded sideways until the first quarter earnings in May, when Western Union had indicated that its price increases during the quarter were working. It increased guidance and the stock rose 5 percent.

Table 10.1
Western Union transaction economics

	2007	2008	2009	2010	2011	2012	2013 (Q1)
Transaction fees	3,286.6	3,532.9	3,373.5	3,434.3	3,580.2	3,545.6	872.0
No. of transactions (millions)	167.7	188.1	196.1	213.7	225.8	230.98	55.44
Percent change	14.0%	12.2%	4.3%	9.0%	5.7%	3.0%	(2.0)%
Fee ($/transaction)	19.60	18.78	17.20	16.07	15.86	15.35	15.73
Percent change	(5.8)%	(4.2)%	(8.4)%	(6.6)%	(1.3)%	(3.2)%	2.5%
Agent fees	(1,966)	(2,165)	(2,012)	(2,085)	(2,171)	(2,279)	(2,252)
Agent fees per transaction	(11.7)	(11.5)	(10.3)	(9.8)	(9.6)	(9.9)	(9.8)
Unit profit per transaction	7.88	7.27	6.94	6.31	6.24	5.48	5.94
Percent change	(14.7)%	(7.7)%	(4.6)%	(9.0)%	(1.2)%	(12.1)%	8.3%

Source: Western Union SEC filings.

This new information could undermine my thesis in the short term, and I looked at the impact of price increases on their transaction volumes as well as its competitors' volumes. MGI and Xoom, Western Union's rivals, had reported 11 percent and 51 percent increases in their transaction volumes, respectively, during the first quarter of 2013, while Western Union reported a 2 percent volume decline. It seemed like the competition was taking shares from Western Union and I did not fold.

In July, Western Union stock was up 20 percent since my short recommendation and I seemed to be wrong on my value trap thesis. I told my clients that I would wait until second-quarter 2013 earnings results to review my thesis. Xoom and MGI reported earlier than Western Union, posting solid transaction growth of 57 percent and 14 percent, respectively. Later,

Western Union reported a 3 percent increase in transactions and its stock closed up 1 percent as the market ignored its decline in unit profitability.

I decided to fold from a risk management point of view for a few reasons. Western Union projected transaction and revenue growth in 2014 and hinted at increasing prices in 2014. The stock was now up ~30 percent and could keep rising on these hopes as Western Union continued to buy back shares. Short interest had doubled to ~9 percent and short squeeze now posed a potential risk.

Fold When Growth Exceeds Expectations Consistently and Revisit When the Business Cycle Begins To Inflect

When companies start to build capacity to fulfill an unexpected jump in market demand, they can get carried away and overbuild capacity. Investors can keeping paying up for the stock as long as the order books and sales beat expectations; however, the multiples begin to rerate downward once there is an inflection in the growth curve. It may be a bad idea to predict when the growth rate decelerates or declines and short a stock on that assumption. It is always better to short when there is clear evidence of an interruption in the growth cycle and emergence of clear catalysts, such as competitive and regulatory threats or slowdown in demand. Shorting in absence of visible catalysts can lead to big losses.

CASE STUDY:
TRINITY INDUSTRIES (TRN)

The U.S. shale oil revolution became apparent in 2011 as Bakken Shale in North Dakota and Montana witnessed a huge pickup in oil production. The sudden boom in oil production was a boon for rail car manufacturers, as crude transportation by rail continued to boom in 2012. Oil refiners began ordering oil tankers alongside rail companies, causing tanker cars to be in tight supply. It seemed to be a déjà vu of buildup in railcar capacity during the ethanol boom in 2005. In the ensuing years, the ethanol bubble burst while railcars had built excess capacity.[4]

Trinity Industries was the biggest beneficiary, with its railcar manufacturing and railcar leasing group growing more than 30 percent for six quarters in a row. High operating and financial leverage had helped TRN reach all-time-high operating margins. The company decided to enter a joint venture for its railcar leasing business that would help them boost their order book by an additional billion dollars. I began working on the short case for Trinity after their joint venture announcement in May 2013 as their order backlog seemed unsustainable. WTI and Brent crude oil spreads were at an all-time-high of $20 per barrel, making the transportation of crude by rail economically feasible. However, as Bakken oil became more accessible, the spread was also destined to narrow. Railcar leases tend to be short term and were prone to cancellations if the spread narrowed.[5]

I suspected that railcar manufacturers would face investigations and tighter regulations after a rail car carrying crude oil exploded in Lac-Mégantic, Quebec, turning it into a war zone. Pipelines had always been considered a safer alternative to haul oil; however, new pipeline constructions were delayed and the Keystone pipeline faced environmental hurdles. I published my short thesis in absence of a clear catalyst as I believed that the concerns with railcar manufacturing would eventually surface. I was proved wrong for the next two quarters as continued railcar demand from Trinity's leasing joint venture helped grow its order book.[6] I closed my short position in December 2013 after the stock moved up 20 percent, as there were no signs of any regulatory investigations.

Trinity continued to see strong demand in 2014 and the stock rose another 70 percent by June 2014. A Guardrail whistleblower case, filed in 2012 against Trinity, had just resulted in a mistrial. The whistleblower had accused Trinity of making secret changes to one of its highway guardrail products, which caused them to impale rather than slow vehicles. However, the U.S. Department of Transportation proposed new rules to redress safety risks in July 2014, following a string of fiery train accidents. There was now a visible catalyst, and it seemed a better time to short Trinity.

On October 21, 2014, a federal jury found Trinity guilty in the whistleblower case and ordered Trinity to pay $525 million in damages to the U.S. government. The stock fell 12 percent on the news and was down 33 percent. We covered half of our short position. WTI and Brent crude oil spreads had also narrowed to $2 amid a glut of oil supply, slowing down crude-by-rail demand. Oil prices accelerated their decline in November and December, and Trinity stock fell another 20 percent. We covered our remaining position.

Hot Stocks, High Short Interests: Stay Away from Crowded Shorts

A short squeeze drives up the price of a (typically heavily shorted) stock rapidly when shorts are forced to cover their positions in response to positive news (M&A, analyst upgrades, positive company announcements, regulatory short sale bans, etc.), margin calls, and stop losses. Short squeezes are the single biggest risk for short sellers.

In 2008, Volkswagen (VW) stock soared by almost 5x after Porsche announced that it gained control of an additional 31.5 percent of shares through cash-settled options and it intended to increase its stake in VW from 42.6 percent to 74.1 percent (figure 10.1). Porsche's announcement led to the speculation that there was less than 6 percent of VW float available, while 12.8 percent of VW shares were sold short, resulting in a panic demand for covering the VW stock and a short squeeze.[7]

Short sellers pile into companies whose issues are widely understood in the market. They may be motivated to join already-crowded

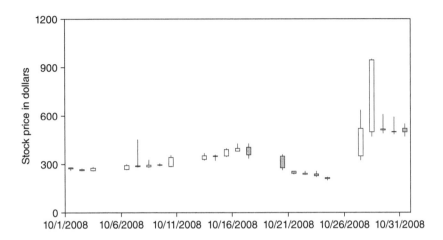

FIGURE 10.1 Volkswagen stock price surges during 2008 short squeeze.
Source: Volkswagen AG 2008 Annual Report, Bloomberg.

shorts on pure speculation or when they cannot find other compelling short ideas. However, crowded shorts have low odds of success because market expectations may already be tempered by weak prospects, and any positive news can lift expectations and squeeze out the shorts.

Rising tides during bull markets can also lift troubled boats. On January 5, 2013, a total of 168 stocks in the Russell 1000 index had a short interest of more than 7 percent, while ~70 percent of them rose an average of 38 percent over the next six months. The odds of success in shorting them would have been less than 30 percent.

Growth Stock, Star CEO: Don't Get in the Way of a Runaway Train!

We have seen many examples of high-growth companies trading at high multiples that can keep expanding. A star CEO, especially a communicative one, can cause the stock price to go up with positive surprises that squeeze short sellers. It is best not to get in the way of such runaway trains; the dangers of shorting based purely on high valuation are quite apparent.

It is the short sellers' word against the star CEO's. The market can rightfully vote for the CEO when it is difficult to handicap the company's growth and there are no immediate threats to the company's growth. The market can also give short-term bumps a pass when the CEO can promote a good case that the company is on track with its long-term growth targets.

Investors especially reward premium valuation to firms run by successful serial entrepreneurs and follow them closely from venture to venture. Silicon Valley has created several billion-dollar enterprises in recent decades, to the extent that technology and growth seem to be synonymous. In particular, former PayPal employees—popularly known in the media as the "PayPal Mafia"—have built many billion-dollar companies in the past decade alone, including YouTube and LinkedIn.

PayPal filed for an initial public offering (IPO) after the dot-com bust in September 2001. The IPO occurred on February 15, 2002, for a market cap of ~$1.2 billion. PayPal, an online bill payment service, was a natural extension of eBay's trading platform, as it derived 70 percent of its revenues from eBay.[8] eBay announced that it would acquire them for $1.5 billion in July 2002, within four months of the IPO. Many of the millionaire PayPal employees left eBay to join or back successful startups (table 10.2).[9]

Elon Musk was already a millionaire before serving as the founder and CEO of PayPal from selling Zip2, his first venture, to Compaq computers in 1999.[10] He made $150 million from the PayPal sale in 2001 and went on to make successful bold moves. In 2003, he started SpaceX, a risky rocket venture that NASA selected to demonstrate delivery and return of cargo to the International Space Station. SpaceX was later awarded a $1.6 billion contract to fly cargo resupply missions.[11]

Table 10.2
Prominent PayPal alumni

PayPal alumni	Position	Key ventures they backed or joined
Elon R. Musk	Founder and CEO	SpaceX, Tesla Motors, SolarCity
Peter A. Thiel	CEO and Chairman	Palantir, Corrum Capital, Facebook
Max R. Levchin	CTO	Slide, Yelp
Russel Simmons, Jeremy Stoppelman	Engineering	Yelp
David O. Sacks	EVP, Products	Yammer
Reid G. Hoffman	EVP, Business Development	LinkedIn, Zynga, etc.
Roelof F. Botha	CFO	YouTube
Steve Chen, Chad Hurley	Engineering	YouTube
John A. Malloy	Director	Waze
Keith Rabois	EVP, Business Development	LinkedIn, Slide, Square, Yelp, Xoom, Khosla Ventures

Musk invested $6.3 million in Tesla Motors, an electric car startup, in 2004, and joined as its chairman, eventually becoming CEO in 2008. He remained a primary funding source for Tesla, ending up with a 65 percent stake at the time of the IPO in June 2010. He also invested $10 million in SolarCity,[12] a solar installation startup, in 2006, and joined as its chairman with a ~32 percent stake at the time of IPO in December 2012.

Tesla and SolarCity have been a tale of two heavily shorted stocks since their IPO, and they are constantly featured in media debates about their prospects.[13] Short sellers were skeptical about their business model and remained in a tug of war. The turning point came in 2013 when both introduced financing programs that boosted their growth prospects, steamrolling skeptical shorts. Both Tesla and Solarcity now had a viable revenue model backed by financing.

CASE STUDY:
TESLA MOTORS (TSLA)

Tug of war ends badly for shorts

Tesla introduced Roadster, its first electric car model, in 2006, and began production in 2008 for 900 reserved orders. Tesla was saved from death in the 2008 financial crisis by a $50 million investment from Daimler in exchange for a 10 percent stake. Meanwhile, the U.S. Department of Energy (DoE) approved a $465 million loan to Tesla that allowed it to raise its production target from 800 per year in 2008 to 20,000 per year in 2012. Tesla priced two new Roadster models above $100,000 and delivered a total of 1,063 cars before their IPO on June 29, 2010.[14]

Tesla had also received 2,200 orders by its IPO for its newly announced Model S—a new four-door model eligible for a federal tax credit of $7,500—with prices expected to start at $49,900. Tesla raised $226 million in the IPO, also attracting $50 million from Toyota, and the stock debuted ~40 percent above the IPO price at $23.89. Short sellers expected Tesla to not make profits until it began shipping the Model S in 2012. They believed that Tesla was also underestimating the cost of production and competition from incumbents. In their opinion, Tesla was overestimating the market size based on reports that estimated electric-based markets would grow 6x to 10.6 million in 2015.

Tesla had delivered a total of 2,150 roadsters at the end of 2011 since it first began deliveries in 2008, while it expected to deliver 5,000 Model S vehicles within six months of commencing production in June 2012. Short sellers were skeptical and won the first round when Telsa had production hiccups in September 2012. Tesla also made a follow-on offering of $128 million, in which Musk offered to buy $1 million of shares.

Tesla produced 3,100 Model S cars in 2012, falling shy of its target to produce 5,000 cars. However, it announced soon after that it had reached its production run rate target of 20,000 per year in December 2012. Short sellers had missed the big picture as production uncertainties cleared and paved the way for Tesla to announce additional capacity of 10,000–15,000 per year for the new Model X. Tesla was optimistic about ending its streak of losses.

Tesla had a banner year in 2013 and its growth continued to be tough to handicap. Musk probably saw it coming when he said in an interview with Fox Business on September 13, 2012: "It was a huge mistake to short Tesla stock and there is a tsunami of hurt coming for those shorting Tesla stock." Shorts were steamrolled amid a barrage of news that followed, rocketing Tesla stock up more than 4× to $180 (figure 10.2).

The shorts were not ready to give up on Tesla after three Tesla cars were reported to have caught fire. A flurry of media stories followed, while images of these burning Tesla cars were constantly replayed on television. Musk got back in action on controlling the damage as the drivers involved in these accidents posted positive stories. The drivers said they could have been dead in any other car, and Tesla gave them enough warning to pull over and get out before the fire caught on. The stock recovered, but the shorts did not let up.

The next leg of short thesis evolved when Musk announced the plan to build the world's largest battery factory, with an investment of $5 billion. Tesla announced that it was selling at least $1.6 billion of convertible notes to finance the project and was entering into a partnership with Panasonic, the biggest supplier of lithium-ion cells used in Tesla batteries. Shorts found new ammunition as they pointed out the risks of failure as evident in the recent

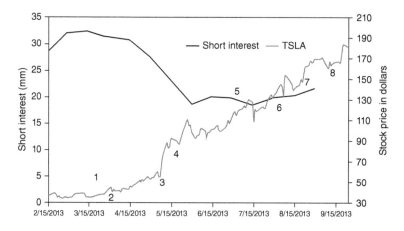

FIGURE 10.2 Key news flow for Tesla stock. *1*, Tesla schedules press conference to reveal financing program; *2*, analysts are skeptical that the
financing will invigorate demand; *3*, Tesla posts adjusted first-quarter
profits, 5,000 Model S vehicles sold in the quarter; *4*, Tesla makes $1 bil-
lion follow-on offering to repay DOE loans; *5*, Goldman analyst downgrades Tesla, says stock defying gravity; *6*, Tesla reports second-quarter
results, 5,150 Model S vehicles beat its own target of 4,500; *7*, Tesla
rises 6 percent on filing trademark for a Model E name; *8*, Deutsche
Bank analyst upgrades price target to $200. *Source:* Tesla press releases,
Bloomberg.

bankruptcies of battery companies. The other concern was that
there was not enough demand for batteries that could provide the
economies of scale and bring down the battery cost. The stock fell
30 percent again.

I was speaking on a short-selling panel at the New York Society
for Securities Analysts on May 9, 2014 (what would have been Ben
Graham's 120th birthday). Tesla stock had just hit a low on the
ongoing concerns on that day and my co-panelists laid down their
case for shorting Tesla. One of them had initiated a small short
position on Tesla in 2013 and believed that Tesla had now become
an attractive short.

I disagreed with my co-panelists because the biggest risk to Tesla's short thesis was betting against Elon Musk, who has a spec-
tacular record of delivering on every big risk he took. Musk was
directly involved with six multibillion dollar companies that he

founded or co-founded. While a couple of these companies went through near-death experiences, they ultimately prevailed. Simple Bayesian math would point to the low odds of successfully betting against Musk, and my only point was not to bet against him.

Failing Ship, Star Captain: Management Star Power Can Revive Stocks

We have seen in previous examples that even star captains can fail to turn around their ships when their industry enters a declining period and products lose relevance amid emerging alternatives. However, their star power has high odds of success when the issues are endemic to the company and not the broader industry. Let us consider the technology industry in particular.

The technology industry has the most dynamic competitive landscape of all industries. It is rare to find tech companies holding a monopolistic grip on their markets for long periods, while it is common to find them losing their dominance to disruptive technologies. Some tech companies spend on innovation (which shows up as research and development expenses on the income statement), while others buy innovative companies (which shows up as capitalized items on the balance sheet). Both strategies are critical to staying ahead or even staying in the race!

Tech companies usually generate a lot of cash, which they constantly reinvest in core research and expensive acquisitions of innovative concepts, but they are often left floundering with their cash after they lose key executives. They can end up as value traps after burning cash in a string of poor acquisitions and failing products; however, it can be dangerous to short them after they have dashed market expectations. Markets can place renewed hope in their salvage if they can hire a star captain.

CASE STUDY:
YAHOO! (YHOO)

Executive turnover, fifth time is the charm

Yahoo! is probably the most fitting example of a fallen angel since it lost the dominance in search engines to Google and failed to acquire them in 2002. Since then, Yahoo! missed out on many key acquisitions, such as Facebook, and made poor acquisitions, such as GeoCities. Yahoo! stock dropped after rejecting an unsolicited bid from Microsoft in 2008, and it remained a value trap for the next four years.

Yahoo! probably saw everything go wrong that could go wrong since then, while the rest of the tech industry witnessed home runs from many startups and rivals. Yahoo! replaced five CEOs in the next four years, lost its grip on its valuable stake in Alibaba, and failed in executing restructuring plans. Yahoo! stock stemmed the decline in 2012 after resolving its dispute with Alibaba and announcing stock buybacks; however, its real tailwind came from hiring Marissa Mayer, a Google alumni. Market expectations lifted on the announcement of her appointment as the new Yahoo! CEO.

Mayer pursued her alma mater's core strategy of aggressive acquisitions, buying more than a dozen companies, including the big-ticket acquisition of Tumblr. Analysts expressed skepticism of her strategic goals, while investors placed hope in her Google pedigree. Yahoo! stock rose more than 70 percent within Mayer's first year as CEO, even as Yahoo! showed dismal growth in revenues or profits.[15]

Hidden Options: Value Waiting to Be Unlocked

Hidden options in a company's business model can sometimes unlock value that is worth many times the stock price. Such options are even more valuable when the company has a strong distribution network to render its products or services. In such a case, a company's speed to deliver new products and services is only constrained by the time needed to develop or acquire new products. Markets can undervalue the distribution network and other hidden options when investor sentiments about the stock turn sour.

CASE STUDY:
NETFLIX (NFLX)

Netflix stock had risen ~7× to $295 since 2009, steamrolling short sellers (including a few reputed ones). In July 2012, Netflix announced price hikes and new subscription plans as part of the plan to separate their DVD rental and online streaming services. Netflix customers were outraged by the price hike and the inconvenience of logging onto two separate websites. Media and analysts launched a series of tirades over this announcement for the next couple of months, forcing the Netflix CEO to apologize; however, the apology seemed too little and too late. Netflix had basically shot themselves in the foot, causing the stock to drop more than 70 percent in a span of four months.

There was no end to the bad news for the stock. Netflix decided to raise $400 million in fresh capital in November 2011 by selling convertible debt at a strike price of $85.8. The stock continued to swing up and down in the following months and ended up trading around $60. Netflix was a consensus short by July 2012. Threats to the Netflix business model from Amazon, CoinStar, and Walmart were a hot discussion topic. News show guests were highlighting how content owners wielded power and Netflix had struggled to renegotiate their video content deals. The popular view seemed to be that content owners had rendered the content aggregation business model useless. Netflix seemed doomed.

I had followed Netflix for a number of years. It piqued my interest when market bears thought the Netflix business model was broken and the stock was going to head even lower after it had swooned 70 percent. Bears were basically arguing that Netflix was a value trap and their subscriber base of 23 million members was now on the path of secular decline.[16] I began evaluating the short thesis on Netflix to find any catch with this value trap argument: Did Netflix not have any hidden value with its 23 million subscribers?

Beware of the Hidden Option in Netflix: Hulu[17]"

I had a Netflix online subscription for $9.99 a month at home and I had just signed up for Hulu Plus. I was watching *The Daily Show with Jon Stewart* on Hulu Plus and was irritated by the fact that Hulu served me with advertisements every few minutes. I was paying $7.99 a month and was expecting a Netflix-like commercial-free treatment.

I became curious about how much Hulu earned from advertisements. While Hulu was a private company owned by Disney, Fox, and Comcast, the Hulu CEO regularly posted its revenue and subscriber numbers in his company blog. It was interesting to note that Hulu users were complaining about advertisements in response to the blog posted by Hulu's CEO.

Hulu made $420 million in 2011, with an average of 1 million paid subscribers, and had ended the year with 1.5 million subscribers. Their revenue math seemed simple, with an $8 per month subscription plan, and subscription revenues came to $96 million (12 months × $8/month × 1 million subscribers). Where did the remaining revenues of >$300 million ($420 million—$96 million) come from? The answer was in-video advertisements, sold on a cost per impression or cost per mille basis.

YouTube had effectively built the in-video advertisement market, although Google, its parent company, had not separately disclosed YouTube's revenues. Street analysts had estimated that YouTube held a lion's share (more than 80 percent) of the $3 billion online video advertisement market. This market was expected to grow 50 percent for the next three to five years.

What Did In-Video Advertisement Mean for Netflix?

In-video advertisement was a real option for Netflix, and it was important to evaluate the value of this real option to determine whether Netflix was a value trap. If Netflix could launch new tiered ad-based pricing for 2 million subscribers (<10 percent of 23 million current subscribers), it could easily generate $600–800 million of incremental advertisement revenues based on Hulu's historical results. Netflix would not need a sizeable investment to launch such a plan and they could generate 50–60 percent in incremental operating margins (~$400 million in incremental net income). At a price-to-earnings ratio of 15–20, the value of the advertising option was >$6 billion. The stock could easily double.

Netflix had two other real options: venturing into in-house content production and introducing a pay-per-view model to watch movies. Both options had the potential to boost Netflix's content library. While Netflix had reported slowing subscription growth in their online streaming business, there were no alarming signs of a decline in the subscription base.

Netflix did not seem like a value trap from any angle. I recommended that my clients buy Netflix in August 2012.

How Did Netflix Play Out?

On October 13, 2012, Hulu borrowed money to buy back 10 percent of their shares for $200 million, valuing them at $2 billion, which implied a valuation of more than $1,000 per subscriber. The transaction seemed expensive, probably because the deal did not involve an outside investor. However, the economics of this transaction implied a valuation of <$200 per subscriber for Netflix, which had a much larger subscription base of 23 million.

On October 31, 2012, Carl Icahn announced in a Securities and Exchange Commission filing that he had recently bought Netflix stock and call options that could give him control of 9.98 percent of the company. Netflix stock soared 20 percent on the news. Five days later, Netflix adopted a poison pill, limiting noninstitutional investors to a 10 percent stake in Netflix shares.

Markets shrugged off any concerns of a tug of war between Carl Icahn and Netflix management and became increasingly optimistic about a possible turnaround. Netflix stocks continued to rise amid optimism about their upcoming earnings on January 22, 2013. Netflix announced surprise positive earnings, an increase in subscribers, and positive earnings outlook. Netflix shares jumped ~40 percent on the news to $146.86 and continued to rise for the next six months, closing at $257.26 on July 12, 2013.

Recap

- Optimal allocation and prudent risk management limit downside, whereas analyzing developments since the initial investment is critical to making allocation changes and risk management decisions.
- Hold on to your position when the story does not change materially. Fold when the story unfolds with unexpected material developments. Revisit thesis when a material catalyst appears. Stay away from crowded shorts: hot stocks with high short interests.
- Do not underestimate the ability of a star CEO.
- Do not get in the way of an early-stage growth stock run by a star CEO when you cannot handicap growth.
- Management star power can move stocks when issues are endemic to the company and not the broader industry. Beware of hidden options that companies can exercise to unlock value.

The Mechanics of Short Selling

Knowledge is better than practice without discernment.
— GITA

THE MECHANICS OF SHORTING STOCKS and buying stocks are different. Shorting a stock is a combination of borrowing shares and selling them in the market. Borrowing stock introduces additional consideration to the trade, such as borrowing fees, the lender calling back their shares, dividend payouts, short squeeze, voting rights, and regulatory restrictions. Most importantly, borrowing stock adds the margin and callable features to the short trade—the most critical risks that make shorting different from simply selling a stock that you own.

In general, the holding period of a short sale trade is shorter than that of a long trade. Short sellers sell stocks that they do not own and the trade is subject to the stock lender's call. Consequently, it is important to identify near-term catalysts or events that can negatively impact the stock.

Simply put, buying a stock is like running a marathon where the finish line is the most important milestone. In comparison, shorting a stock is like a hurdle race, where short-term hurdles (getting called on the stock, merger and acquisition rumors, short-sale restrictions, etc.) are as important as the finish line.

It is also possible to enter a long (buy) or short (sell) trade without buying or selling the actual stock. Derivatives such as options, futures, and swaps offer alternatives to trading stocks or cash equities. Derivatives are geared toward more sophisticated investors because gains and losses involved in trading derivatives can be much higher than in trading stocks. I will cover some basics of options in this chapter as well.

Takeaway
Shorting is risky because it involves borrowing. When you short a stock, the lender can force you to cover (or close) your position on short notice and force you to realize losses at an inopportune time.

Key Differences Between Shorting and Buying

Opening the Short Position

You can open a long position and buy as many shares as you want, depending on the stock's liquidity (volume traded). In comparison, a normal short sale requires you to locate and preborrow the stock so it can be delivered to the buyer within the standard three-day settlement period and avoid a failure to deliver. In other words, you cannot short sell a stock unless someone has first promised to lend it to you.

Short selling has long been blamed for stock market abuses, especially during the Great Depression. In 1934, Congress directed the Securities and Exchange Commission (SEC) to purge the market of short selling abuses. The SEC adopted restrictions on short selling in a stock while the price was falling. That rule remained unchanged for more than sixty years until the adoption of Regulation SHO in 2004 to curb naked short selling.[1] *Naked short selling* refers to selling the shares without borrowing them first or ascertaining that the stocks are available to borrow.

Regulation SHO requires broker-dealers to close out all failures to deliver in threshold securities that exist for thirteen consecutive settlement days. Threshold securities are equity securities that have an aggregate fail-to-deliver position for five consecutive settlement days, total 10,000 shares or more, and are equal to at least 0.5 percent of the issuer's total shares outstanding. Exchanges update information on the threshold securities list on a daily basis and on short interest (number of short-sold shares outstanding) on a biweekly basis.

You may have identified your best short idea, but you will not be able to short the stock if it is not available to borrow due to high demand or short sale restrictions. In such a case, costs can be abnormally high for stocks that are available to borrow. Derivatives may be the only alternative left in such a case, and puts are the most common derivatives used for shorting.

While it may still be possible to place derivative trades (options, swaps, or futures) on the underlying stock, such trades can be crowded as well, making the derivatives expensive and lowering the expected returns on short investments. The price of derivatives, such as puts, depends not only on the underlying stock price but on many other moving parts (time of expiration, stock volatility, and interest rates, etc.) that can further lower returns.

BUYING PUTS IS LIKE BUYING INSURANCE

Buying a put option is similar to buying automobile insurance. The insured pays a premium for automobile collision and liability and gets the right to claim for damages in the event of an accident. Similarly, when you buy a put option on a stock, you pay a premium to protect (or hedge) your stock investment.

How Does a Put Option Work?

Suppose you have 100 shares of Company X that is trading at $120 per share and you fear that X shares may fall by $10 to $20 in the next six months. You do not want to sell your X stock at $120 per share; however, you want to protect your losses. In other words, you want the (put) option to sell X at $120 per share over the next six months if X falls. You decide to buy such an option (traded on the options exchange as a put option) at the prevailing market price of $2 per share or $200 for one contract (one contract is usually based on 100 shares).

A few months later, your fears come true: X is trading at $105 and you lose $15 per share on the stock; however, your put option compensates for this loss by allowing you to sell X at $120 per share. Alternatively, you can decide to keep X and sell the put instead for a premium of $15 per share ($120 minus $105). Had X stock traded above $120 per share, you would have lost the $2 premium.

Do You Really Need to Own X's Stocks to Buy a Put Option?

Not really. Unlike automobile insurance, which requires you to own the car before you can buy the insurance, a put option does not require you to own the stock. In that case, you would actually profit from the falling stock, akin to shorting the stock.

Put Option and Shorting: Risk Versus Reward

The idea behind shorting or buying put options is to profit from falling stocks; however, the rewards and risks involved are a little different. As discussed, when you buy a put option, your maximum loss is the premium paid. The returns on a put option can be multifold. For example, you made $13 per share on a $2 per share put option (a whopping 6.5× or 650 percent return).

In contrast, if you had shorted 100 shares of X stock at $120, the notional value of the short investment is $120 × 100 = $12,000. Your broker will typically retain the entire proceeds and may require you to keep 30 percent (or $3,600) as initial margin, depending on regulatory requirements. In this case, your return will be lower at 41.67 percent ($1,500 on $3,600).

However, what if X stock went up $15 or $30, or doubled? The risk seems unlimited here as compared to the limited risk of losing the premium when you buy puts. Buying puts seems like a better proposition in this case, but not always. The price of a put option (or premium) depends on many factors other than the stock price.

The premium for a put option also depends on the volatility, time period, prevailing interest rates, and strike price (the price at which you want to sell the stock). Volatile stocks will demand higher put premiums, and a six-month option will be pricier than a three-month option. A higher strike price (the price at which you would like to sell the stock) will demand higher premiums.

Higher premiums resulting from such factors increase the cost of investment. On top of this, the stock must fall by the value of the premium before the put expires to break even on the trade. Because you can lose 100 percent of the premium on bad trades, a string of bad trades can severely cripple your portfolio.

Closing the Short Trade

In the absence of margin or borrowed money, cash equities holders can theoretically hold onto their stocks forever. However, short sellers can be forced to close their positions in the face of adverse events—lender calls, regulatory restrictions, short squeeze, and margin shortfalls, to name a few.

It is important to understand that the lender continues to be the owner of stock that they lend the short seller to short. It gets a little trickier after the short seller sells the stock, because we now have a second owner of the stock. For example, if 20 percent of a company's outstanding stocks are sold short, 20 percent of the stocks are held by the lender, and another 20 percent is held by the new owners who bought these shares from the short seller. Thus, short selling in this case lowers the float (stocks available to trade) from 100 percent to 60 percent (100 percent minus 20 percent minus 20 percent).

Does it get more complicated if the founder or a strategic owner has a 60 percent stake in the company? It not only becomes trickier but extremely risky for the short seller, because the float now lowers to 0 percent (60 percent minus 60 percent). Even if a small percentage of the lenders decide to recall their shares, they can squeeze short sellers, forcing them to find and buy back shares. Positive stock news can also force short sellers to cut losses and cover their position

BUYING CALLS IS A SHORT SELLER'S INSURANCE

Buying a call option allows you to lock the stock price at the desired price (or strike price). The buyer pays a premium for this price insurance, and gets the right to buy the stocks at the strike price in the future. Such insurance can be a lifesaver for the short seller, should the shorted stock keep rising.

How Does a Call Option Work?

Suppose you have shorted 100 shares of X that is trading at $120 per share. You fear that any positive earnings or new acquisition announcements by X can drive up their shares by $10 to $20. You do not want to cover your X stock; however, you want to protect your losses in the event the stock rises. In other words, you want the (call) option to buy X at $120 per share over the next six months if X stock rallies. You decide to buy such an option at the prevailing market price of $2 per share or $200 for one contract (one contract is usually based on 100 shares).

A few months later, X is trading at $135 and you lose $15 per share on your short position; however, your call option compensates for this loss by allowing you to buy X at $120 per share. Alternatively, you can decide to keep X short and sell the call instead for a premium of $15 per share ($135 minus $120). Had X traded below $120 per share, you would have lost the $2 premium.

When you buy a call option, your maximum loss is the premium paid, similar to a put option. The returns on a call option can be multifold. For example, you made $13 per share on a $2 per share put option (a whopping 6.5x or 650 percent return). In contrast, if you had bought 100 shares of X stock at $120, your returns will be lower at 12.5 percent ($1,500 on $12,000).

Call Option Versus Shorting

Selling a call option is somewhat similar to shorting stocks because you are betting that the stock price will not go up. In the previous example, you collect a $2 premium when you sell a call option and you can keep this premium if the stock does not rise above $120. However, if X rises to $135, you lose $13 per share.

When you sell the X call option, your maximum profit is the $2 premium collected, even if X stock falls by $10 per share. In contrast, a short position stands to make a profit of $10 per share in this case.

Duration or Holding Period of Shorts

Due to the callable nature of a short trade (the lender has the option to recall their shares), adding short positions to a stock portfolio lowers the duration or holding period of the portfolio. An untimely recall on the shorts can lead to unwanted losses. While it may be difficult to eliminate this timing risk, the right short position size (less concentrated positions) can mitigate the size of the loss.

Investment Hurdle Rate and Payoff

In the absence of margin, the investment hurdle rate for a stock is zero or its benchmark index. However, short investments have an investment hurdle rate of at least the borrowing cost and the stock dividend yield in addition to the fund benchmark. Short-only funds can invest the cash proceeds from the stock in the fund benchmark or the market to eliminate benchmark risk.

The payoff for short investments is almost the mirror opposite of long investments. The maximum upside for a short idea and maximum downside for a long idea are 100 percent. Conversely, the maximum downside for a short idea and maximum upside for a long idea are theoretically unlimited. In Warren Buffett's words, "You can't make big money shorting because the risk of big losses means you can't make big bets."[2] Short interest may be only one side of the story.

Short sales may not necessarily be motivated by a bearish opinion on the stock. Pair trading, arbitrage, and market-making activities also constitute a large part of short trading volume and short interest. It is nearly impossible to get insight into the long counterparts of a short leg for these trades. For example, if a money manager discloses that he or she is short on a copper stock, it is hard to tell if the money manager is hedging homebuilder stocks or bearish on copper.

Lack of Disclosure on Who Is Short on the Stock

Short interest statistics indicate the level and change in short activity for a stock, but not the players behind the short bets; however, prominent short sellers often reveal their short positions. On the other hand, stockholding reports provide more color on the stock owners, their level of holdings, and recent changes to holdings (table 11.1).

Table 11.1
Google short interest

Settlement date	Short interest	Average daily share volume	Days to cover
September 14, 2012	3,524,796	2,681,179	1.314644
August 31, 2012	4,118,402	2,189,948	1.880594
August 15, 2012	4,180,876	2,224,799	1.879215
July 31, 2012	3,903,004	2,955,335	1.320664
July 13, 2012	3,835,260	2,257,680	1.698762

Source: Bloomberg.

Tax Treatment Is Mostly Short-Term Gain or Loss

Short sale gains and losses are treated mostly as short term, but they can sometimes be treated as long term based on the amount of time the stock is held before it is delivered to the lender to close the short trade. Tax treatment of dividends paid on shorts is subject to holding period requirements, which can restrict you from deducting dividends paid on short positions held for less than 46 days but allow you to increase the basis of covering stock.

Takeaway
Shorting is different from buying stocks in many respects, including the mechanics, tax treatment of potential profits or losses, and hurdle rate.

Common Types of Short Equity Funds

Common types of short equity funds include the long-short hedge fund, short-only or short-biased fund, 130/30 long-short mutual funds, and short and ultra-short exchange-traded funds.

Shorting Is Not for Everyone

The discipline of short selling is not suited for an average individual investor; it is geared more toward institutional investors with sophisticated research and risk management resources.

Hedge funds dominate in short strategies and their charter mandates them to short stocks. They offer both short-only and long-short products. Mutual funds and exchange-traded funds (ETFs) that traditionally offered long-only products have begun offering long-short funds (e.g., 130/30 or 150/50) and short-only ETFs in the last five years.

Short sellers are up against many factors: asymmetric returns, squeeze risk, short-term capital gain treatment, and borrowing costs, among others. Their interests often clash with everyone in the market—promoters, Wall Street analysts, renowned investors, and even regulators.

So, what is the motivation for institutions behind shorting? Good shorting strategies promise to protect downside and potentially deliver positive returns, allowing money managers to generate positive returns—even during bear markets.

Recap

- Shorting involves borrowing stocks in order to sell short.
- Borrowing makes shorting risky because the lender can force you to cover (or close) your position on short

notice and force you to realize losses at an inopportune
time.

- Derivatives, such as options and futures, offer alternatives to stocks or cash equities. Puts are the most common derivatives used for shorting.
- Buying puts is akin to shorting stocks. Buying calls lowers the risk of shorting stocks by providing protection against a surge in stock price. Selling calls is a poor substitute for shorting.
- Short squeezes are the single biggest risk for short sellers.
- Shorting is different from buying stocks in many respects: mechanics, potential profits and losses and their tax treatment, and hurdle rates.
- Shorting is geared toward institutional investors with sophisticated research and risk management resources.
- Long-short hedge funds, 130-30 mutual funds, and ultra-short ETFs are the most common investment funds that short stocks.

Glossary

ADJUSTABLE RATE MORTGAGE (ARM) Mortgage with a fixed rate for an initial period, which can be two years, five years, seven years, or ten years. Mortgage rate resets to floating rate at the end of the initial period of fixed rates.

AVERAGE REVENUE PER UNIT (ARPU) A commonly used key performance indicator (KPI) in the telecom industry for revenue generated from the sale of one cell phone.

ASSET-BACKED SECURITIES (ABS) ABS security is derived from securitization of assets such as car loans and credit card receivables. (*See* Securitized product)

BLACK-SCHOLES PRICING MODEL Companies use this popular mathematical model to price European-style derivative instruments (e.g., employee stock options, warrants, and convertible bonds).

CATALYST Events or news that can trigger a positive or negative reaction to the stock price. Investors and analysts like to identify and watch catalysts (earnings, product launches, restructuring, management changes, monthly retail sales, capacity expansion, etc.) to time their buy or sell decisions.

COLLATERALIZED DEBT OBLIGATIONS (CDO) A subset of asset-based securities (ABS) that can be based on loans, bonds, commercial real estate, structured products, or synthetic obligations from derivatives, such as credit default swaps and other CDOs.

COMP STORE SALES (also referred to as comps, comp sales, same store sales, like store sales) Typically refers to the revenue growth for stores that have been open for a year or more. Many retail companies report comp store sales on a monthly basis, and some report on a quarterly or annual basis. Comp sales is a closely watched number for retail stocks.

CREDIT DEFAULT SWAP (CDS) CDS instruments allow investors to short bonds with limited downside, just like put options on equities. CDSs are identical to insurance contracts on bonds or loans that are issued by corporations or sovereign entities. A CDS contract holder pays a fixed premium to the seller, and the seller agrees to pay the face value of the loan or bond if the issuer defaults. An issuer default may not necessarily mean bankruptcy or insolvency, but it can trigger a credit event when the bond issuer fails to meet certain loan service conditions or indentures (e.g., failure to pay interest or maintain a certain ratio of profitability in relation to its obligations).

A CDS is an over-the-counter (OTC) financial instrument traded mostly by institutional investors and investment banks. A typical contract may be based on an International Swaps and Derivatives Association (ISDA) Master Agreement and customized to specific investor needs. CDSs were launched in the 1990s, but caught public attention during the financial crisis of 2008.

CDX An index of CDSs similar to the S&P 500 index for stocks. CDX can be based on investment grade credit, high yield credit, or other credit securities. CDX and ABX (an index of subprime mortgage-backed securities) came to prominence during the financial crisis when a handful of investors made successful short bets on these indices. CDX and ABX can provide insurance protection on credit instruments.

CYCLICALITY The correlation of company sales to expansionary or recessionary cycles of the economy. Once economic recovery begins after an economic recession, early-cycle stocks such as financials tend to recover first, followed by mid-cycle stocks such as industrials, and then late-cycle stocks such as materials and energy. Defensive stocks such as utilities and consumer staples tend to outperform during recessionary phases.

D/E (Debt/Equity) AND D/C (Debt/Capital) D/E is the ratio of long-term liabilities to the book value of equity, and D/C is the ratio of long-term liabilities to total capital (liabilities + equity). D/E or D/C indicate the indebtedness of the company and are also called leverage ratios. Leverage ratios and debt service ratios are important indicators of indebtedness of a company.

DAYS TO COVER The number of days it would take for all short sellers to cover their positions; the calculation is based on the average trading volume of the stock. If average daily volume of a stock is 3,000,000 and the number of shares sold short is 6,000,000, it would take two days to cover the entire short position. Days to cover is also called short ratio.

(DEBT + CAPITALIZED LEASE)/EBITDAR When a company has long-term operating lease contracts, debt/EBITDA does not depict its true ability to service the debt. In such a case, debt can be adjusted to include the capitalized lease and rental expense can be added back to EBITDA. Analysts typically use 8× rental expense as a proxy for capitalized lease. A debt/EBITDA ratio below or close to 1 can be an alarming signal.

DISCOUNTED CASH FLOW (DCF)/NET PRESENT VALUE (NPV) DCF and NPV techniques project future cash flows of a company and discount them to the present value to determine the value of the stock. This discounting technique is based on the concept of the time value of money; i.e., the value of a dollar today is worth more than a dollar tomorrow. DCF valuation rests on two critical assumptions: (1) revenue and earnings projections, and (2) discount rate or cost of equity. PV10 is a commonly used DCF valuation technique in the oil and gas industry where cash flows are discounted at a fixed rate of 10 percent.

DIVIDEND DISCOUNT MODEL (DDM) Projects future dividends of a company and discounts them to the present value to determine the value of the stock. This model is used for mature companies with a long history of dividends.

Earnings per Share (EPS) A closely watched number and strong driver of stock prices. EPS = net income/shares outstanding, and is also known as basic EPS or trailing EPS (net income for the trailing one year is used here). Diluted EPS calculation adjusts shares outstanding for any dilution from issuance of employee options, warrants, etc.

Forward EPS = consensus net income/shares outstanding. Consensus net income is the average net income for the next year or future years as estimated by Wall Street analysts.

Normalized EPS = normalized net income/shares outstanding. Net income is normalized to eliminate one-time charges or extraordinary items.

EV/EBITDA Takes overall debt, cash balance, and minority interests into account and ignores depreciation and amortization as operating costs. It is a commonly used valuation multiple in capital intensive and leveraged industries.

EV/(EBITDA–CAPEX) Depreciation and amortization are non-cash expenses based on a company's estimated life of the related assets. Companies assume the value of an asset goes to zero or a salvage value, and expense that value as depreciation costs over the asset's estimated life. However, some or most of this depreciation cost may be real since companies need to make capital investments every year. Companies may seem cheap if the EBITDA is not adjusted to reflect these investments (or Capex). EBITDA-Capex adjusts for recurring investments to provide a better measure of operating profitability for industrial companies or hard asset intensive companies.

FILINGS The Securities and Exchange Commission (SEC) is a primary regulator for U.S. stocks and mandates companies to file certain forms periodically to disclose material information (information that is highly likely to impact stock price).

FLOAT Shares outstanding that are available to trade. Stock with 40 percent float means 60 percent of the stocks are closely held by insiders, institutions, etc., and are not available to trade in the public market.

FREE CASH FLOW (FCF) MULTIPLE OR YIELD Free cash flow is defined as net operating profits after tax (NOPAT) + depreciation and amortization (D&A) minus change in net working capital minus capital expenditures. FCF is excess operating cash generated by the company after capital expenditures. FCF yield = FCF/market cap and FCF multiple = market cap/FCF. Companies can use FCF to buy back shares or pay special dividends. In theory, a company trading at 20 percent FCF yield or a 5× FCF multiple (1/20) can buy back all its shares in five years. High FCF yields indicate that the stock is trading cheap but can often also lead to value traps.

FREE FLOAT This approach to valuing insurance companies was popularized by Warren Buffett. Free float refers to the assets available from net claims liabilities under insurance contracts. Buffett makes the argument that these liabilities are available free of cost for insurance companies (with strong underwriting history) to invest in capital markets. The major components of float are unpaid losses, life, annuity and health benefit liabilities, unearned premiums and other liabilities to policyholders less premium and reinsurance receivables, deferred charges assumed under retroactive reinsurance contracts, and deferred policy acquisition costs.

INITIAL PUBLIC OFFERING (IPO) The initial public offering of shares in a private company that decides to sell its shares to the general public. IPO underwriters (investment banks) are responsible for allocation and pricing of the shares. IPO shares in the United States are allocated at the offering price, mostly to institutional investors.

LEVERAGE The magnitude of a company's borrowings. Leverage or gearing (commonly used leverage ratios are D/C, D/E, Debt/EBITDA) measures a company's indebtedness resulting from interest-bearing loans. Leverage can also result from large-scale operations or high fixed costs.

MARGIN Profitability expressed in percentage terms. For example, gross margin = gross profit/revenues, operating margin = operating profit/ revenues. MARGIN STOCKS refer to stocks bought on loan from a stockbroker. Initial and maintenance margin (collateral deposit against portfolio) refer to the initial and maintenance deposits needed to buy or short stocks and derivatives.

OFF-BALANCE SHEET LIABILITIES Commitments and contingencies that are reported separately from the balance sheet, such as special notes and disclosures, and can result in additional borrowings.

PAY-IN-KIND (PIK) These stocks or bonds pay interest or dividends in the form of additional stocks or bonds, instead of cash payments.

Price/Book (P/B) The ratio of market capitalization to book value of equity. A P/B ratio of less than 1 indicates that the stock is cheap, and high P/B ratio indicates strong earnings growth or high return on equity (ROE). P/B is commonly used to value banks, insurance companies, and capital intensive or leveraged industries

Price/Earnings (P/E) or Price/Earnings per Share (EPS) The most commonly used valuation metric. A P/E multiple of 10 means that the investor is willing to pay $10 per share per $1 of EPS last year. In general, low P/E indicates that the market expects a lower earnings level, and high P/E indicates that the market expects growth in earnings. P/E for a company with growth expectations will be much higher than 10x and can reach ridiculous levels (100x to 500x) depending on hype and the market's mood. Forward P/E is the ratio of stock price and forward EPS (or consensus).

P/FFO Similar to the FCF multiple for REITs. FFO (funds from operations) can also be adjusted for capital expenditures for a better picture.

Price to Sales (P/S) Can be a useful valuation metric for unprofitable companies. High growth companies and cyclical companies may sometimes produce low or negative earnings. In such a case, P/E, EV/EBIT, etc. may need to be normalized and P/S may be the right valuation multiple to use.

Price per Subscriber (P/Sub) or Enterprise Value per Subscriber (EV/Subscriber) A commonly used metric in telecommunications, media, and internet businesses.

P/E to Growth (PEG) This ratio is used for high growth companies. PEG adjusts P/E for earnings growth. A PEG ratio less than 1 could indicate that the growth stock is trading cheap.

PUT OPTIONS Similar to auto insurance. The insured pays a premium for auto collision and liability and gets the right to claim for damages in the event of an accident. Similarly, when you buy a put option on a stock, you pay a premium to protect (or hedge) your stock investment. A put option does not require you to own the stock and can be used as an alternative way to short stocks.

REAL ESTATE INVESTMENT TRUST (REIT) A trust that invests in real estate and mortgages and is required to distribute more than 90 percent of its taxable income to its investors.

REAL OPTION VALUATION The valuation of real options embedded in a stock. Real options are projects that a company can possibly undertake or discontinue; for example, launch of a new product or service, divestment of an unprofitable business segment, or expansion of production capacity. Valuation of hidden options and projects is especially important for short sellers because stocks can rocket up when companies exercise such options.

RETURN ON INVESTMENT (ROI) Profits expressed as a percentage of assets, equity, and invested capital. Returns help investors understand the impact of leverage and operating scale. Attractive businesses tend to have high overall returns. Returns of more than 10 percent over a 5-year period usually point to good business economics.

ROA = NET INCOME/TOTAL ASSETS

ROE = NET INCOME/TOTAL EQUITY

ROIC = NET INCOME/INVESTED CAPITAL

SEASONALITY The cyclical variation of revenues during a calendar year. For example, retail sales tend to peak in December due to Christmas sales. Natural gas demand tends to peak during winter, and oil demand peaks during summer, impacting the revenues and margins of refiners and oil companies.

SECURITIZED PRODUCTS Securitization is the process of converting nontradable loans, such as mortgages and car loans, to tradable securities called securitized products.

SHAREHOLDER DILUTION Companies may issue employee stock options, warrants, convertible debt, and other derivatives that may result in issuance of additional shares. Consequently, company earnings must be shared with these new shareholders, resulting in dilution of existing shareholders.

SHORT INTEREST The total number of short-sold shares outstanding, often expressed as a percentage of shares outstanding or as a ratio of float. Exchanges update this information on a biweekly basis.

SHORT SQUEEZE Rapid driving up of the price of a (typically heavily shorted) stock when shorts are forced to cover their positions in response to positive news (mergers and acquisitions, analyst upgrades, positive company announcements, regulatory short sale bans, etc.), margin calls, and stop losses. Short squeezes are the biggest risk for short sellers.

SOVEREIGN CDS Equivalent to buying insurance on a government bond.

SPIN-OFF Separation of a parent stock corporation into two or more separately tradable stocks. Spin-offs are typically noncash, tax-efficient transactions where the parent company may distribute new shares in the resulting spin-off to existing shareholders.

SUM OF THE PARTS (SOTP) VALUATION Used to value conglomerates or companies with multiple business segments operating in different industries. For example, Berkshire Hathaway operates in various industries including insurance, reinsurance, utilities, and freight rail transportation segments. Each of the business segments can be valued separately using valuation methods relevant to its industry, and the right value of Berkshire Hathaway should be the sum of the value of each of these parts (or segments).

SWITCHING COST A tangible or intangible measure of the brand strength of a company. Switching cost may refer to the actual monetary cost for a consumer to switch from one brand to another, or to the inconvenience or wasted effort in switching brands.

TED SPREAD The difference between short term T-bills (short-term government borrowing) and LIBOR rates implied by short-term Eurodollar (ED) futures. LIBOR is the interbank borrowing rate and also serves to gauge the systemic banking risk. Any sharp increase in LIBOR reflects high credit risk in the banking system. During a crisis, investors tend to flock to Treasury securities and push down the Treasury yields, further widening the TED spread. Calculation: If a 3-month Eurodollar contract is trading at 97.5, the implied LIBOR = 100 minus 97.5 = 2.5 percent. If 3-month Treasury bills yield 0.5 percent, the TED spread is 2 percent or 200 basis points per share.

TERM STRUCTURE A graph showing the relationship among interest rates of Treasuries with different maturities. An upward slope usually indicates economic expansion while a downward slope indicates recession.

VALUE TRAP Like fallen angel stocks whose glory days may not come back as a result of structural changes in their business or the industry. Value traps tend to trade at low valuation multiples (e.g., P/B, P/E) and their multiples can stay depressed for long periods.

VIX (the Fear Index) A measure of implied volatility of 30-day options on the S&P 500. A VIX reading of 20 indicates an expected annualized move of 20 percent in S&P 500 over the next 30 days. VIX hit an all-time high of ~90 in October 2008, after the Lehman Brothers collapse. VIX tends to trade between 10 and 20 during periods of complacence and shoots up amid market worries.

ZONE OF INSOLVENCY Companies are said to be in the zone of insolvency when they begin to tread close to their credit covenants and show signs of distress. A company in the zone of insolvency may be pushed into bankruptcy by any additional distress, such as a sudden fall in operating profits or values of assets, or a steep increase in funding costs.

Notes

1. Due Diligence in Short Selling

1. Chanos, J. (2003, May 15). *Prepared statement for panel discussion on "Hedge Fund Strategies and Market Participation."* Retrieved from http://www.sec.gov/spotlight/hedgefunds/hedge-chanos.htm

2. U.S. Congressional Hearing (2008, November 13). *Hedge funds and the financial markets.* Retrieved from https://house.resource.org/110/gov.house.ogr.20081113_hrs15REF2154.1.pdf

3. Tilson, W. (April 2001). *Notes from the 2001 Berkshire Hathaway Annual Meeting.* Retrieved from http://www.tilsonfunds.com/motley_berkshire_brkmtg01notes.php

4. Cisco Systems (1998–2001). *Form 10-Ks and 10-Qs.* Retrieved from http://www.sec.gov/edgar.shtm

5. Questcor Pharmaceuticals (2010–2012). *Form 10-Ks and 10-Qs.* Retrieved from http://www.sec.gov/edgar.shtm

2. Leveraged Businesses: The Upside and Downside

1. Eastman Kodak (2011). *Form 10-K.* Retrieved from http://www.sec.gov/edgar.shtm

2. Office Depot (2009). *Form 8-K.* Retrieved from http://www.sec.gov /edgar.shtm

3. IATA (2008). *Press release.* Retrieved from http://www.iata.org/press room/pr/Pages/2008-29-05-02.aspx

3. Structural Issues in Industries

1. AIG (2006). *Annual report.* Retrieved from http://www.aig.com /Chartis/internet/US/en/2006-10k_tcm3171-440889.pdf

2. U.S. Department of Housing and Urban Development. *Subprime lending.* Retrieved from http://portal.hud.gov/hudportal/HUD?src=/program _offices/fair_housing_equal_opp/lending/subprime

3. Carpetright PLC (2006–2012). *Annual reports, interim statements, and presentations.* Retrieved from http://www.carpetright.plc.uk/investors

4. Boston Consulting Group (2010, March 2). *Projecting U.S. Mail Volumes to 2020.* Retrieved from http://about.usps.com/future-postal-service /gcg-narrative.pdf

5. Solar Energy Industries Association. *Solar investment tax credit (ITC).* Retrieved from http://www.seia.org/policy/finance-tax/solar-investment-tax -credit

4. Recipes for Cooked Books: Accounting Misstatements and Shenanigans

1. U.S. General Accounting Office (October 2002). *Financial statement restatements: Trends, market impacts, regulatory responses, and remaining challenges.* Retrieved from http://www.gao.gov/new.items/do3138.pdf

2. Incyte Corp. (2012, April 26). *First quarter 2012 press release.* Retrieved from http://investor.incyte.com/phoenix.zhtml?c=69764&p=irol -newsArticle_pf&id=1687652

3. Apple Inc. (2010). *Form 10-K.* Retrieved from http://www.sec.gov /edgar.shtm

4. Tesla Motors (2012). *Form 10-K.* Retrieved from http://ir.teslamotors .com

5. Financial Accounting Standards Board (2013, May 16). *IASB and FASB propose changes to lease accounting.* Retrieved from http://www.fasb .org/cs/ContentServer?pagename=FASB%2FFASBContent_C%2FNewsPag e&cid=1176162614474

6. Skechers USA Inc. (2011, May 5). *Form 10-Q*. Retrieved from http://skx.com/investor.jsp?p=2

7. Garmin International Inc. (2008). *Form 10-K*. Retrieved from http://www.garmin.com/en-US/company/investors/sec/form-10-K

8. HP (2012, November 20). *Press release*. Retrieved from http://www8.hp.com/us/en/hp-news/press-release.html?id=1334263

9. The Walt Disney Company (2012). *Form 10-K*. Retrieved from http://thewaltdisneycompany.com/sites/default/files/reports/q4-fy12-form-10k.pdf

10. Marvell Technology (2012, December 27). *Press release*. Retrieved from http://www.marvell.com/company/news/pressDetail.do?releaseID=3296

5. The World Is Going to End

1. BBC News (1998, December 6). *The man who broke the Bank of England.* Retrieved from http://www.bbc.co.uk/search/news/?page=3&q=george%20soros%201992&dir=fd&news=41&news_av=1

2. Bernanke, B. (2003, May 31). *Some thoughts on monetary policy in Japan, remarks by Governor Ben S. Bernanke.* Retrieved from http://www.federalreserve.gov/boarddocs/speeches/2003/20030531/

3. Bernanke, B. (1994). *The Macroeconomics of the Great Depression: A Comparative Approach.* Working Paper No. 4814. Retrieved from http://www.nber.org/papers/w4814.pdf?new_window=1

4. Bernanke, *Some thoughts on monetary policy.*

5. Lattman, P. (2011, June 23). *Regions settles S.E.C. action and puts a unit up for sale.* Retrieved from http://query.nytimes.com/gst/fullpage.html?res=9E01EFDE103EF930A15755C0A9679D8B63&ref=regionsfinancialcorporation

6. Regions Finance (2009–2011). *Annual reports, quarterly reports, presentations.* Retrieved from http://ir.regions.com/

7. Matthews, D. (2013, October 9). *Seventeen academic papers of Janet Yellen's that you need to read.* Retrieved from http://www.washingtonpost.com/blogs/wonkblog/wp/2013/10/09/seventeen-academic-papers-of-janet-yellens-that-you-need-to-read/

8. Yellen, J. and Akerlof, G. (2004). *Stabilization policy: A reconsideration.* Retrieved from http://www4.fe.uc.pt/jasa/m_i_2010_2011/stabilizationpolicyreconsideration.pdf

6. Value Investing

1. Graham, B. and Dodd, D. (2009). *Security Analysis*. Sixth Edition (New York: McGraw-Hill).
2. Kahn, I. and Milne, R. (1977, May 4). *Benjamin Graham: The Father of Financial Analysis, Occasion Paper Number 5*. Retrieved from http://www.cfapubs.org/doi/pdf/10.2470/rf.v1977.n1.4731
3. Graham and Dodd, *Security Analysis*.

7. Activist Investing

1. George, B. and Lorsch, J.W. (2014, May). *How to outsmart activist investors*. Retrieved from http://hbr.org/2014/05/how-to-outsmart-activist-investors/ar/

8. Papa Bear: Coattailing Marquee Investors or Betting Against Them?

1. Einhorn, D. (2010, December 10). *Fooling some of the people all of the time: A long short (and now complete) story*. Retrieved from http://foolingsomepeople.com/main/
2. Richardson, K., Lucchetti A., and Pleven, M. (2008, February 1). "Bond insurer's woes add to credit-market stress." *The Wall Street Journal*. Retrieved from http://online.wsj.com/article/SB120175741480431553.html
3. Banco Popular (2006–2010). *Form 10-Ks and 10-Qs*. Retrieved from http://www.sec.gov/edgar.shtm
4. Kucera, D. (2012, May 16). "Einhorn Says Amazon's future a 'riddle' as profit lags sales." *Bloomberg*. Retrieved from http://www.bloomberg.com/news/2012-05-16/einhorn-says-amazon-s-future-a-riddle-after-profit-lags-sales.html
5. Bezos, J. (2012). *Annual Letter to Amazon Shareholders*. Retrieved from http://phx.corporate-ir.net/phoenix.zhtml?c=97664&p=irol-reportsannual
6. Apollo Group (2009–2011). *Form 10-Ks and 10-Qs*. Retrieved from http://www.sec.gov/edgar.shtm

9. Off Wall Street: Two Decades of Successful Shorting

Off Wall Street contributed its original research to be reproduced in this book.

1. Lieberman, J. (2002, Feb. 27). *The watchdogs didn't bark: Enron and the Wall Street analysts.* Retrieved from http://www.gpo.gov/fdsys /pkg/CHRG-107shrg78622/pdf/CHRG-107shrg78622.pdf

10. When to Hold, When to Fold

1. Western Union (2012–2013). *Annual Reports, Quarterly Reports, Presentations.* Retrieved from http://ir.westernunion.com/

2. XOOM (2012–2013). *Annual Reports, Quarterly Reports, Presentations.* Retrieved from http://ir.xoom.com/

3. MoneyGram (2012–2013). *Annual Reports, Quarterly Reports, Presentations.* Retrieved from http://ir.moneygram.com/

4. Nunez, C. (2014, July 23). *As fiery accidents pile up, U.S. proposes new rules for oil trains.* Retrieved from http://news.nationalgeographic .com/news/energy/2014/07/140723-united-states-oil-train-rules-proposed/

5. Lee, P. (2014, July 19). *Trinity guardrail whistle-blower case results in mistrial.* Retrieved from http://www.bloomberg.com/news/2014–07–19 /trinity-guardrail-whistle-blower-case-results-in-mistrial.html

6. Ivory, D. and Kessler, A. (2014, October 20). *Guardrail maker Trinity Industries liable for fraud in Texas.* Retrieved from http://www .nytimes.com/2014/10/21/business/jury-says-trinity-industries-a-highway -guardrail-maker-defrauded-us.html?_r=0

7. Marsh, S. (2008, October 28). *Short sellers make VW the world's priciest firm.* Retrieved from http://www.reuters.com/article/2008/10/28/us -volkswagen-idUSTRE49R31920081028

8. eBay (2002, July 8). *Press Release.* Retrieved from http://investor.ebay.com /releasedetail.cfm?releaseid=84142

9. Rosmarin, R. (2006, July 12). *The PayPal exodus.* Retrieved from http:// www.forbes.com/2006/07/12/paypal-ebay-YouTube_cx_rr_0712paypal .html

10. Friedman, J. (2003, April 27). *Zip2 and PayPal pioneer prepares for latest launch.* Retrieved from: http://articles.chicagotribune.com/2003–04–27 /business/0304260304_1_space-exploration-technologies-corp-elon-musk-paypal

11. SpaceX *About SpaceX.* Retrieved from http://www.spacex.com/about

12. Marshall, M. (2006, September 15). *Musk leads $10M Investment in SolarCity.* Retrieved from http://venturebeat.com/2006/09/15/musk-leads -10m-investment-in-solarcity-to-provide-solar-for-all/

13. SolarCity (2012–2013). *Form S-1, 10-K, 10-Q, and Investor Presentations.* Retrieved from http://amda-14lqre.client.shareholder.com/index.cfm

14. Tesla Motors (2010–2013). *Form S-1, 10-K, 10-Q, Blogs, and Investor presentations.* Retrieved from http://ir.teslamotors.com/

15. Yahoo! (2000–2013). *Form 10-K, 10-Q, and Investor Presentations.* Retrieved from http://amda-14lqre.client.shareholder.com/index.cfm

16. Netflix (2009–2012). *Annual Reports, Quarterly Reports, Presentations.* Retrieved from http://ir.netflix.com

17. Kilar, J. (2012, January 12). *2011, 2012 and beyond (Hulu CEO Blog).* Retrieved from http://blog.hulu.com/2012/01/12/2011-2012-and-beyond/

11. The Mechanics of Short Selling

1. Securities and Exchange Commission (2003, November 13). *Proposed new regulation SHO.* Retrieved from http://www.sec.gov/rules/proposed /34-48709.htm

2. Strauts, T. (2012, August 22). *Don't sell yourself short.* Retrieved from http://ibd.morningstar.com/article/article.asp?id=565378&CN=brf295,http:// ibd.morningstar.com/archive/archive.asp?inputs=days=14;frmtId=12,%20 brf295

Index

holding strategy: F5 Networks case
study on, 190–91; on hidden
options, 204–8; on material
developments, 189–91; Netflix
case study on, 205–8; poker
analogy of, 187; recap, 208; on
star executives, 197–204; Tesla
Motors case study on, 200–203,
202; Yahoo! case study on, 204
hotel industry, 93
Housing and Urban Development
(HUD), 63
Howard Hughes, 149
HP. *See* Hewlett-Packard
HSBC, 43, 64
HUD. *See* Housing and Urban
Development
Hulu, 206
Hurd, Mark, 29
hurdle rate, 216
Hurley, Chad, *199*

Icahn, Carl, 159, 207
IMF. *See* International Monetary
Fund
incentive structure: of hedge funds,
5, 124, *125*; leverage and lack
of, 45–46; operating metrics and,
92, 94
income statement divergence, 87–88
Incyte, 82–83
industrials metrics, *93*
industry: analysis components, 11;
competition and struggling, 46,
46–47; cyclical versus secular
trends, 25–27; leverage-dependent,
56–57; operating metrics trends
specific to, 91–92, 93
industry structural issues. *See*
broken growth; value traps
insider transactions, 18–20
Instagram, 34
insurance industry: Ackman issue-
spotting in, 151–52; AIG value

trap case study, 61–63, 65–66,
66; call options like, 214; MBIA
in, 62, 145, 149, 151–52, 158;
Medicare/Medicaid, 20–22,
30–31; monolines in, 62, 151;
operating metrics, 93; put
options like, 211–13
intangible assets, 85
The Intelligent Investor (Graham),
119, 121, 126
interest coverage ratio, 91
International Monetary Fund
(IMF), 141
Internet: Amazon.com, 78–79,
165–68, *166*; AOL, 32, 178–79;
auction marketplaces, 181–82,
198; dot-com bubble, 8–10, 32;
eBay, 198; Facebook, 32–34;
Google, 34, 70, 204, 217;
holding strategy case study on,
190–91; messaging apps, 33,
34; mobile advertising, 32–34;
Netflix, 205–8; newspaper
industry and, 25–26, 71, 133;
PayPal alumni, 198, *199*;
photo sharing, 33, 34; retail
disruption by, 71–72; search, 70;
video, 205–8; Yahoo!, 70, 204;
YouTube, 206
interviews. *See* investor interviews
inventory: accounting, 83, 84–85;
turnover, 90
investigations: Ackman firm, 158;
Allied Capital, 157; as catalyst,
15, 17–18; Diamond-Pringles, 17;
Herbalife, 150, 152; Office Depot,
44; SoGen International, 127
investment tax credits (ITCs), 74
investor interviews: with Ackman,
145–54; with Eveillard, 126–42;
with Roberts, 171–80. *See also*
Buffett, Warren; Graham, Ben
investors: announcements by,
18–20; meetings with, 28–30

Roberts, Mark: accolades for,
171–72; on accounting
misstatements, 178–79;
background of, 172–74; early
ideas of, 174, 178–79; on
follow-ons and high profile, 181;
on holding or folding, 179; on
macroeconomics, commodities
and value traps, 180; on
repeated shorting, 179–80;
research evolution of, 175; on
short strategies, 177–81; on
short versus long ideas, 176–77
Rodriguez, Bob, 136
runaway determination, 175,
197–200
Russell 1000 index, 197

Sacks, David O., *199*
safety, margin of, 122, 123–24, 146
sales: accounts receivables, 85, 90;
costs, 84
sale-type leases, operating leases
versus, 83
salvaged asset auctions, 181–82
Sanborn Map, 143
S&P. *See* Standard & Poor
SEC. *See* Securities and Exchange
Commission
secular trends, cyclical versus,
25–27
Securities and Exchange
Commission (SEC): abuse
restrictions by, 210–11; Ackman
firm investigation by, 158; Allied
Capital investigation by, 157;
Diamond-Pringles investigation
by, 17; form filing with of, 18;
Herbalife investigation by, 150,
152; Office Depot investigation
by, 44; Regions Financial
settlement with, 107; Regulation
FD of, 28; responsiveness of,
152; SoGen International fund
investigation by, 127

Security Analysis (Graham), 11,
120
sell-in versus sell-through, 82–83
Shakespeare, William, 38
shale oil, 57, 194–95
Shapland, Darren, 69
shareholders: creditors versus,
in bankruptcy or liquidation,
40–41; dilution example, 45
shipping industry: leverage
dependence of, 56; postal value
traps in, 71
short equity funds, 218
short ideas. *See* due diligence
short selling: abuses, 210–11;
Ackman on, 150; activist
investing on, 146–47, 149;
Buffett on, 3, 123, 134; call
options versus, 214–15;
categories of, 13–15, 16; closing
trade in, 213–15; crowded, 155–
56, 159, 160, 196–97; dividends
taxes, 217; duration or holding
period for, 215, 217; equity
funds, 218; Eveillard on, 132–
37; fundamental analysis aspects
for, 10–13; Graham on, 120–21;
long investing versus, 146–47,
149, 176–77; mechanics recap,
218–19; naked, 211; opening
trade in, 210–13; players, 216;
put options versus, 211–13;
repeated, 179–80; Roberts on,
176–81; success recap, 182–83;
suitability for, 218; types of,
209–10; value investing versus,
123–24, 130–31, 134–35
Simmons, Russel, *199*
SIVs. *See* structured investment
vehicles
Skechers, 85
smartphone makers, 22–23
Smith Barney, 127
Snapchat, 33
Société Générale, 126–27, 128–29

www.ingramcontent.com/pod-product-compliance
Ingram Content Group UK Ltd.
Pitfield, Milton Keynes, MK11 3LW, UK
UKHW042233220225
455398UK00010B/161/J